# Approaching Performance Assessments with Confidence

*By Carol Jago*

In order to get good at anything, you need to practice. Whether the goal is to improve your jump shot, level up in a video game, or make the cut in band tryouts, success requires repeated practice on the court, computer, and field. The same is true of reading and writing. The only way to get good at them is by reading and writing.

Malcolm Gladwell estimates in his book *Outliers* that mastering a skill requires about 10,000 hours of dedicated practice. He argues that individuals who are outstanding in their field have one thing in common—many, many hours of working at it. Gladwell claims that success is less dependent on innate talent than it is on practice. Now I'm pretty sure that I could put in 10,000 hours at a ballet studio and still be a terrible dancer, but I agree with Gladwell that, "Practice isn't the thing you do once you're good. It's the thing you do that makes you good."

Not just any kind of practice will help you master a skill, though. Effective practice needs to focus on improvement. That is why this series of reading and writing tasks begins with a model of the kind of reading and writing you are working towards, then takes you through practice exercises, and finally invites you to perform the skills you have practiced.

Once through the cycle is only the beginning. You will want to repeat the process many times over until close reading, supporting claims with evidence, and crafting a compelling essay is something you approach with confidence. Notice that I didn't say "with ease." I wish it were otherwise, but in my experience as a teacher and as an author, writing well is never easy.

The work is worth the effort. Like a star walking out on the stage, you put your trust in the hours you've invested in practice to result in thundering applause. To our work together!

# PERFORMANCE ASSESSMENT

Houghton Mifflin Harcourt

9

Printed in the U.S.A.

ISBN 978-0-544-56936-2

2 3 4 5 6 7 8 9 10   0928   22 21 20 19 18 17 16 15

4500547447       A B C D E F G

# Unit 1 Argumentative Essay
# Relationships

## STEP 1 ANALYZE THE MODEL

*Is it better to be at the center of one group of friends or at the perimeter of several?*

### Read Source Materials

## STEP 2 PRACTICE THE TASK

*Is reaching consensus always a good idea, or are there times when it is better to disagree?*

### Read Source Materials

### Write an Argumentative Essay

## STEP 3 PERFORM THE TASK

*Can you make real friends on the Internet?*

**Read Source Materials**

# Unit 2 Informative Essay
# Ancient Civilizations

## STEP 1 ANALYZE THE MODEL

*Exploring Peru*

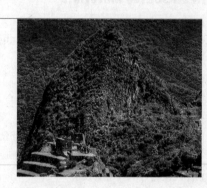

**Read Source Materials**

## STEP 2 PRACTICE THE TASK

*In what ways are the Mayan and Egyptian pyramids alike and different?*

### Read Source Materials

### Write a Comparison/Contrast Essay

## STEP 3 PERFORM THE TASK

*In what ways were the Maya, the Aztecs, and the Inca advanced for their time?*

### Read Source Materials

### Write an Informative Esssay

# Unit 3 Literary Analysis
## Changes

# Unit 4 Mixed Practice
# On Your Own

# Relationships

# UNIT 1

# Argumentative Essay

## STEP 1
### ANALYZE THE MODEL

*Evaluate an argumentative essay about whether it is better to have many friends or a few close friends.*

## STEP 2
### PRACTICE THE TASK

*Write an argumentative essay that evaluates the benefits and drawbacks of reaching a consensus.*

## STEP 3
### PERFORM THE TASK

*Write an argumentative essay that offers reasons for or against making friends on the Internet.*

Questioning another person's point of view is something we as humans love to do. Interacting with others—friends, neighbors, relatives, strangers—sometimes can lead to disagreements. Arguing, giving your reasons for your stance on an issue, and explaining your point of view, can be challenging on a person-to-person level.

The argumentative essay, on the other hand, is a more formally constructed argument.

**IN THIS UNIT,** you will learn how to write an argumentative essay that is based on your close reading and analysis of several relevant sources. You will learn a step-by-step approach to stating a claim—and then organizing your essay to support your claim in a clear and logical way.

*Is it better to be at the center of one group of friends or at the perimeter of several?*

## You will read:

▶ **TWO INFORMATIONAL ARTICLES**

*New School, New Groups of Friends*

*Teen Friendships: A Cauldron of Closeness*

## You will analyze:

▶ **A STUDENT MODEL**

*Are Close Friends Better?*

# Source Materials for Step 1

The following texts were used by Ms. Jefferson's student, Philip Patel, as sources for his essay, "Are Close Friends Better than Many Friends?" As you read, make notes in the side columns and underline information that you find useful.

**NOTES**

# New School, New Groups of Friends

It was really tough moving and starting from scratch at a new school, but after a year, I can say that there have been some good things as well as bad ones.

At my old school, I was part of a small group of "band geeks." That's what we called ourselves because that's what we were. I was right at the center of the group. I helped decide things like what we were going to do for fun, where we would sit in the lunchroom, and who we would hang out with. I'm not saying we were a clique but we knew each other really well and all agreed that we didn't want a lot of random kids hanging out with us.

The problem with a group like that is that it is hard to change and try new things without your friends getting mad at you or thinking you are rejecting them. So, at my new school, I've made an effort not to get too tight with any one group, but to try new things and stay flexible. I like being involved with a few groups and getting to know kids with different interests, even if I'm not right at the center of things. It's a relief not to have to worry about any of the intense friendship drama and just have fun doing cool activities and meeting new people.

I certainly miss my old gang of friends, but it's been a lot of fun having this chance to spread myself out.

# Teen Friendships:
## A CAULDRON OF CLOSENESS

It will come as no surprise to parents that the teenage years are particularly intense ones when it comes to friendships and group dynamics. Many of our children find themselves both benefitting from—and sometimes struggling with—issues relating to being part of a group of friends.

Being part of a small, tight group can bolster a teen's sense of identity, supply a feeling of belonging, and provide close, loyal, and lasting friendships. Being part of a group can mean fewer awkward social moments, fewer social decisions to make, and more social stability and security.

Problems arise when a group becomes too small, too closed and limiting, or too controlling. The teenage years are times of great change and growth, and children should be free to rethink themselves and their friendships without the limitation of what can amount to a group veto.

Being the center of a tightly knit group can mean that there is less freedom to explore, meet new friends, and try out other interests and ideas. It is important that children understand that even the best of friends sometimes grow apart. They may no longer share the same interests. It is normal, natural, and healthy to change and grow, and even sometimes grow apart.

Maintaining a variety of friendships, some close, and some more casual, can help a teen through a tough transition out of a group. Also, it is important to remind teens to conduct themselves in a manner that they will have no cause to regret later on, always being fair, upfront, and generous. People of all ages do well when they remember that being right isn't as important as being kind.

### Discuss and Decide

You have read two sources about social circles. Without going any further, discuss the question: Is it better to be at the center of one group of friends or at the perimeter of several? Cite text evidence in your discussion.

# Analyze a Student Model for Step 1

Read Philip's essay closely. The red side notes are the comments that his teacher, Ms. Jefferson, wrote.

Philip Patel
Ms. Jefferson
English 9
November 18

# Are Close Friends Better?

*Interesting hook.*

Do I really have to choose? If I could have my way, I would have both. I'd be at the center of a small group of close friends, but I'd also have a wide range of more casual friendships. Being at the perimeter of a number of groups would be a good balance to my more intense and cliquish small group. I'd have depth as well as breadth, and I'd have options if anything ever went wrong in my small group.

*The issue and your claim are clear.*

But let's say I can't have both and I have to choose one. In that case, I would choose to be at the center of a group of friends, even if that group were only three or four people. Here's why: no number of casual friends can equal the benefit of having one or two true close friends. Close friends are nothing like casual friends. You can trust them. You can laugh with them. They are there for you when life is good and when it is tough.

*Good transition.*

*Valid reason, clearly stated.*

Also, being at the center of something is completely different from being on the outside. When you are in the center of a small group of friends, you have a say over things. You can say what you prefer and what you really think. You can make decisions, or help make decisions. You are in charge.

*Excellent point.*

When you are on the perimeter of a group, you are on the outside looking in. You can decide to join in or not, but you can't really participate in decision-making, and that can get frustrating.

*Valid opposing claim.*

1. Analyze    2. Practice    3. Perform

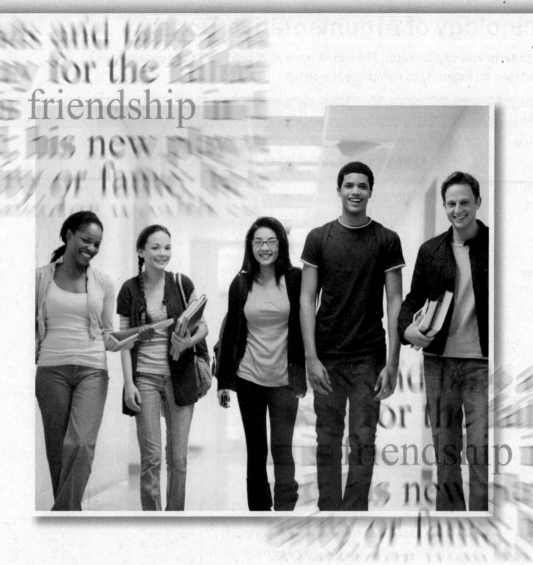

It is nice to know people from many different groups with many different interests, but if none of them are close friends, then you are still missing out.

It's true that being at the center of a small group is like putting all your eggs in one basket. Yes, it has more risks, but it also has more rewards. There is nothing quite as special as a group of close friends.

*Concluding statement is well made.*

*Well done!*

## Discuss and Decide

Did Philip's essay convince you that it is better to have a small circle of friends? If so, which of his reasons are the most compelling?

# Terminology of Argumentative Texts

Read each term and explanation. Then look back at Philip Patel's argumentative essay and find an example to complete the chart.

| Term | Explanation | Example from Philip's Essay |
|------|-------------|----------------------------|
| **audience** | The **audience** for your argument is a group of people that you want to convince. As you develop your argument, consider your audience's knowledge level and concerns. | |
| **purpose** | The **purpose** for writing an argument is to sway the audience. Your purpose should be clear, whether it is to persuade your audience to agree with your claim, or to motivate your audience to take some action. | |
| **precise claim** | A **precise claim** confidently states your viewpoint. Remember that you must be able to find reasons and evidence to support your claim, and that you must distinguish your claim from opposing claims. | |
| **reason** | A **reason** is a statement that supports your claim. (You should have more than one reason.) Note that you will need to supply evidence for each reason you state. | |
| **opposing claim** | An **opposing claim,** or **counterclaim,** shares the point of view of people who do not agree with your claim. Opposing claims must be fairly presented with evidence. | |

1. Analyze   2. Practice   3. Perform

*Is reaching consensus always a good idea, or are there times when it is better to disagree?*

## You will read:

▶ **A NEWSPAPER ARTICLE**
*Consensus Will Be Used to Decide School Board Policy*

▶ **AN INFORMATIONAL ARTICLE**
*How to Reach a Consensus*

▶ **A LIST**
*Is Consensus Decision-Making Right for Your Group?*

▶ **TWO LETTERS TO THE EDITOR**

## You will write:

▶ **AN ARGUMENTATIVE ESSAY**
*Is reaching a consensus always a good idea, or are there times when it is better to disagree?*

# Source Materials for Step 2

**AS YOU READ** Analyze and annotate the sources in ways that help you reach a decision regarding consensus.

## Source 1: Newspaper Article

# Consensus Will Be Used to Decide School Board Policy

**by Soledad Stephens, Education Correspondent**                    **May 25, 2012**

At a meeting last night, the Tiberi Township School Board chose a new method to determine standards for grade promotion. Normally the 12-person board votes on the proposals. Now they will use consensus to build a plan of action acceptable to all. Although none are likely to get their first choice, there will also be no winners and no losers.

Consensus decision-making is very different from voting. Voting is a way to choose between alternatives. With consensus, a group can bring the best parts of many proposals together to create something new. Voting is faster, but it may leave some "defeated" voters upset with the outcome. When a group achieves consensus after a thorough discussion, all parties are on board with the outcome.

"I'm just pleased we will be working together to shape a proposal that everyone can get behind," said School Board President Patti Rincon.

However, not all are in consensus about using consensus.

"Consensus is too much compromise," said parent Tyrell Washington. "Everyone gives up something and no one really likes the final result. They should keep working until they have a proposal that everyone likes, unanimously!"

School administrator Jesse VanDeLaar thinks just the opposite. "These decisions should be made by the experts," he declared. "It really isn't useful to vote or reach consensus. This is not a popularity contest—it's a question of what the research has shown will or will not work."

Good luck to the members of the school board on reaching a consensus that will be accepted by all stakeholders—parents, teachers, *and* school administrators.

# How to Reach a Consensus

A *consensus* is when a group of people reaches a general agreement. Getting to a consensus requires a special decision-making process that takes everyone's opinions and concerns into account. In consensus decision-making, everyone is included, everyone participates, everyone's voice is equal, and everyone works towards the same goal—finding a solution.

1. Define and describe the issue that needs to be decided.

2. Decide how your group will reach a final decision. (Some groups insist on unanimity; others accept a consensus with one or two dissenting voices.)

3. List all the concerns that the final proposal should address.

4. Brainstorm and record a list of possible solutions. Encourage every participant to offer ideas, opinions, and comments.

5. Evaluate the list of alternatives. Write up a draft proposal that combines the best of all the ideas.

6. Revise the proposal until it best meets the interests of the group.

## Close Read

You've read two sources on reaching a consensus. Explain some advantages to making decisions this way, and cite text evidence to support your response.

_____

_____

# Source 3: List

## Is Consensus Decision-Making Right for Your Group?

### Advantages of Consensus Decision Making:

▶ Consensus decision-making helps build trust and a sense of community.

▶ Everyone's ideas are included, which leads to a wider range of possible solutions.

▶ The solutions are supported by the whole group.

### Reaching a consensus may be difficult if:

▶ the group has not worked together before or is too large (15 or more).

▶ some members do not understand or accept the consensus-seeking process, or argue, bully, or intimidate others.

▶ the issue is complicated with few viable solutions available.

▶ one member has more power than others (this may discourage others from speaking freely).

▶ there is a lack or trust among group members.

▶ there is not enough time for discussion.

▶ group leaders try to control outcomes rather than facilitate discussion.

▶ one or two "dissenters" hold up the whole process.

▶ there is no agreed-upon consensus process for the group to use.

## Discuss and Decide

When might making a decision by consensus not be the best method to use?

# Source 4: Letters to the Editor

## To the Editor

I'm writing to protest the School Board's recent adoption of the consensus decision-making method to decide grade promotion policy. This is not a situation where it is appropriate to choose a course of action by finding something that everyone can agree on. Maybe everyone agrees on a plan that makes no sense at all. Decisions about grade promotions should be made by administrators who have responsibility and experts who have special knowledge. We owe our students the BEST decisions, not just the most popular ones.

Yours truly,
Jesse VanDeLaar
Deputy Principal

## To the Editor

Congratulations to the School Board for choosing to make their policy decisions by consensus! No longer will the policies they adopt be the subject of bitter disagreements and lackluster support. We parents will no longer feel like cats who have left the mice to play. When the whole school board unites behind a plan, then teachers, parents, and students will unite behind it as well. A plan which has taken into consideration the opinions and interests of all the members—and survived extensive debate—is a plan that will stand the test of time.

In a world with far too much strife and conflict, few leaders seem to have the skills needed to compromise and work together effectively. Hats off to the school board for leading by example.

Mary Anne Dunlop
Parent

## Discuss and Decide

Which claims in one letter are not directly refuted in the other letter?

# Respond to Questions on Step 2 Sources

**These questions will help you analyze the sources you've read. Use your notes and refer back to the sources in order to answer the questions. Your answers to these questions will help you write your essay.**

**1** Evaluate the sources. Is the evidence from one source more credible than the evidence from another source? When you evaluate the credibility of a source, examine the expertise of the author and/or the organization responsible for the information. Record your reasons in the chart.

| Source | Credible? | Reasons |
|---|---|---|
| **Newspaper Article** Consensus Will Be Used to Decide School Board Policy | | |
| **Informational Article** How to Reach a Consensus | | |
| **List** Is Consensus Decision-Making Right for Your Group? | | |
| **Letters to the Editor** | | |

**2 Prose Constructed-Response** If you disagreed with Mary Anne Dunlop's position on decision-making by consensus, which sources would you use to refute her argument? Why?

_____

_____

**3 Prose Constructed-Response** Which source best complements the information found in the list, "Is Consensus Decision-Making Right for Your Group?" Explain your rationale, citing evidence from the text.

_____

_____

# Searching for Evidence

Every reason you offer to support the central claim of your argument must be upheld by evidence. It is useful to think ahead about evidence when you are preparing to write an argument. If there is no evidence to support your claim, you will need to revise your claim. The evidence you provide must be relevant, or related to your claim. It must also be sufficient. Sufficient evidence is both clear and varied.

Use this chart to help you vary the types of evidence you provide to support your reasons.

| Types of Evidence | What Does It Look Like? |
|---|---|
| **Anecdotes:** personal examples or stories that illustrate a point | **Letters to the Editor** "No longer will the policies they adopt be the subject of bitter disagreements and lackluster support." |
| **Commonly accepted beliefs:** ideas that most people share | **Newspaper Article** "'Consensus is too much compromise,' said parent Tyrell Washington." |
| **Examples:** specific instances or illustrations of a general idea | **Newspaper Article** "Normally the 12-person board votes on the proposals. Now they will use consensus to build a plan of action acceptable to all." |
| **Expert opinion:** statement made by an authority on the subject | **Newspaper Article** "'. . . we will be working together to shape a proposal that everyone can get behind,' said School Board President Patti Rincon." |
| **Facts:** statements that can be proven true, such as statistics or other numerical information | **Informational Article** "A *consensus* is when a group of people reaches a general agreement." |

Write an argumentative essay to answer the
question: Is reaching consensus always a good idea?
Are there times when it is better to disagree?

# Planning and Prewriting

Before you draft your essay, complete some important planning steps.

**Claim ➡ Reasons ➡ Evidence**

 You may prefer to do your planning on a computer.

## Make a Precise Claim

**1.** Is reaching consensus always a good idea? Are there times when it is better
to disagree?                                            yes ☐    no ☐

**2.** Review the evidence on pages 10–13. Do the sources support your
position?
                                         yes ☐    no ☐

**3.** If you answered *no* to Question 2, you can either change your position or
do additional research to find supporting evidence.

**4.** State your claim. It should be precise. It should contain the issue and your
position on the issue.

> **Issue:** Decision-making by consensus
>
>
> **Your position on the issue:** _____
>
>
> **Your precise claim:** _____

## State Reasons

Next gather support for your claim. Identify several valid reasons that justify your
position.

| Reason 1 | Reason 2 | Reason 3 |
|---|---|---|
|  |  |  |

# Find Evidence

You have identified reasons that support your claim. Summarize your reasons in the chart below. Then complete the chart by identifying evidence that supports your reasons.

**Relevant Evidence:** The evidence you plan to use must be *relevant* to your argument. That is, it should directly and factually support your position.

**Sufficient Evidence:** Additionally, your evidence must be *sufficient* to make your case. That is, you need to supply enough evidence to convince others

| Short Summary of Reasons | Evidence |
|---|---|
| Reason 1 | Relevant? _____<br>Sufficient? _____ |
| Reason 2 | Relevant? _____<br>Sufficient? _____ |
| Reason 3 | Relevant? _____<br>Sufficient? _____ |

# Finalize Your Plan

Whether you are writing your essay at home or working in a timed situation at school, it is important to have a plan. You will save time and create a more organized, logical essay by planning the structure before you start writing.

Use your responses on pages 16–17, as well as your close reading notes, to complete the graphic organizer.

▶ Think about how you will grab your reader's attention with an interesting fact or anecdote.

▶ Identify the issue and your position.

| Introduction |
| --- |

| Reason/ Evidence | Reason/ Evidence | Reason/ Evidence |
| --- | --- | --- |

▶ State your precise claim.
▶ List the likely opposing claim and how you will counter it.

| Opposing Claim |
| --- |

▶ Restate your claim.

| Concluding Section |
| --- |

1. Analyze    2. Practice    3. Perform

# Draft Your Essay

As you write, think about:

▶ **Audience:** Your teacher

▶ **Purpose:** Demonstrate your understanding of the specific requirements of an argumentative essay.

▶ **Style:** Use a formal and objective tone that isn't defensive.

▶ **Transitions:** Use words, such as *furthermore* or *another reason,* to create cohesion or flow.

# Revise

## Revision Checklist: Self Evaluation

Use the checklist below to guide your analysis.

 If you drafted your essay on the computer, you may wish to print it out so that you can more easily evaluate it.

| Ask Yourself | Tips | Revision Strategies |
|---|---|---|
| Does the introduction grab the audience's attention and include a precise claim? | Draw a wavy line under the attention-grabbing text. Bracket the claim. | Add an attention grabber. Add a claim or rework the existing one to make it more precise. |
| Do at least two valid reasons support the claim? Is each reason supported by relevant and sufficient evidence? | Underline each reason. Circle each piece of evidence, and draw an arrow to the reason it supports. | Add reasons or revise existing ones to make them more valid. Add relevant evidence to ensure that your support is sufficient. |
| Do transitions create cohesion and link related parts of the argument? | Put a star next to each transition. | Add words, phrases, or clauses to connect related ideas that lack transitions. |
| Are the reasons in the order that is most persuasive? | Number the reasons in the margin, ranking them by their strength and effectiveness. | Rearrange the reasons into a more logical order of importance. |
| Are opposing claims fairly acknowledged and refuted? | Put a plus sign by any sentence that addresses an opposing claim. | Add sentences that identify and address those opposing claims. |
| Does the concluding section restate the claim? | Put a box around the restatement of your claim. | Add a sentence that restates your claim. |

# Revision Checklist: Peer Review

Exchange your essay with a classmate, or read it aloud to your partner. As you read and comment on your classmate's essay, focus on logic, organization, and evidence—not on whether you agree with the author's claim. Help each other identify parts of the draft that need strengthening, reworking, or a new approach.

| What To Look For | Notes for My Partner |
|---|---|
| Does the introduction grab the audience's attention and include a precise claim? | |
| Do at least two valid reasons support the claim? Is each reason supported by relevant and sufficient evidence? | |
| Do transitions create cohesion and link related parts of the argument? | |
| Are the reasons in the order that is most persuasive? | |
| Are opposing claims fairly acknowledged and refuted? | |
| Does the concluding section restate the claim? | |

# Edit

 Edit your essay to correct spelling, grammar, and punctuation errors.

# Can you make real friends on the Internet?

## You will read:

▶ **A NEWSPAPER ARTICLE**
*Study: The Internet Helps You Make More Friends, Be More Social*

▶ **A BLOG**
*Social Media, Pretend Friends, and the Lie of False Intimacy*

▶ **A MAGAZINE ARTICLE**
*Making Friends Through the Internet*

## You will write:

▶ **AN ARGUMENTATIVE ESSAY**
*Can you make real friends on the Internet?*

# Study:
# The Internet Helps You Make More Friends, Be More Social

by Graeme McMillan, June 16, 2011

**AS YOU READ** *Analyze the data presented in the articles. Look for evidence that supports your position that you can make real friends online, or inspires you to change your position.*

**NOTES**

It's the kind of news you can use next time concerned parents bring up the idea that the internet is making people more withdrawn and closed off from the rest of humanity: A new study from the Pew Research Center has found that online social networks actually seem to make people more social.

Pew polled 2,255 Americans during October and November last year, and of the 1,787 internet users in that group, 47% used social networking sites. Facebook was used by 92% of the 975 people that used social networks, with MySpace in second place, with 29%.
10 Linkedin and Twitter trailed behind, with 18% and 13% respectively.

That's almost twice as many as in 2008, when the survey was last held. But more interestingly, there's also been a rise in the number of close friendships people are reporting when compared with 2008—2.16 close friends on average, compared with 2008's 1.93—with that increase being lead by those online, who reported an average of 2.26 close friends to the offline respondents' 1.75. It gets even better when you look at those using social networks, who reported 2.45 close friends on average.

## Discuss and Decide

The author includes information about the number of close friends reported. What trend does the Pew Survey seem to reveal? Cite text evidence in your discussion.

> "…online Americans tend to have 664 [social] ties on average, compared with an offline average of around 506."

The study even looked into the number of social ties internet
20 users and non-internet users have, and found that online Americans tend to have 664 ties on average, compared with an offline average of around 506. That number goes crazy when you start to plug in different social networks, however: Facebook users average 648 social ties, but Twitter users have an average of 838.

So, the next time someone says that they think the internet is bad for society, the answer is clear: Sign them up for Twitter, and see how they feel a couple of weeks later.

**NOTES**

## Close Read

**1.** How did Pew Research collect their data?

_____

_____

**2.** Explain the change in the number of people using social networking sites from 2008 to 2011.

_____

_____

**3.** Are the increases in "close friends" and "ties" similar or different? Cite evidence from the text to support your answer.

_____

_____

_____

_____

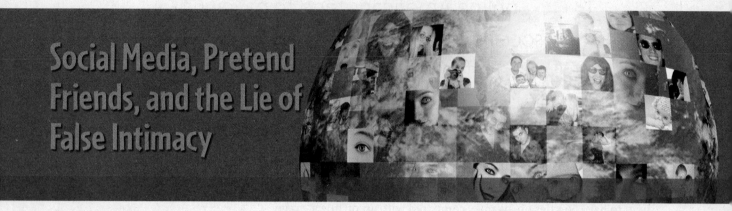

# Social Media, Pretend Friends, and the Lie of False Intimacy

© Houghton Mifflin Harcourt Publishing Company • Image Credits: ©HaywireMedia/Fotolia

**AS YOU READ** *Note all the issues that having many online friends can create. Is your opinion altered by this information?*

**NOTES**

It's not an illusion. We really are doing more with each 24 hours, as technology enables (or forces) us to interact and intersect and do and consume with unprecedented volume and vigor. **We live our lives at breakneck speed because we can, because we feel we have to keep up, and because every macro and micro breeze blows in that direction.**

I remember the days before social media when I would get 20 phone calls per day and 50 or 60 emails, and felt exhausted by the pace of communication. Now we've traded the telephone for other
10  connection points (I only get 2-3 calls per day), but the overall number of people ringing our doorbell through some mechanism has ballooned like Charles Barkley.

**The number of "inboxes" we possess is staggering:** Email (3 accounts for me), public Twitter, Twitter DM, public Facebook, Facebook messages, Facebook chat, Linkedin messages, public Google +, Google + messages, blog comments, Skype, text messages, Instagram, phone, voice mail, and several topically or geographically specific forums, groups and social networks. That's a lot of relationship bait in the water.

## Close Read

Which specific words does the author use in the text to suggest his or her position? What inference can you make about the nature of this position?

_____

_____

1. Analyze   2. Practice   ▼ 3. Perform

**20  The Lie of Opportunity**

How do we justify this? How do we convince ourselves that slicing our attention so thin the turkey becomes translucent is a good idea?

**We do it because we believe that more relationships provides more opportunity.**

*"It's not what you know, it's who you know."*

*"Social media makes a big world smaller."*

*"Linkedin is for people you know, Facebook is for people you used to know, Twitter is for people you want to know."*

**30**    All of these chestnuts are passed around like a flu strain because they make intuitive sense. But common among them is the **underlying premise that interacting with more people is inherently better than interacting with fewer people.** I have always believed this to be true, and in fact have delivered the lines above in presentations and on this blog. But today, I'm no longer convinced.

**Instead I wonder, what if we have it ALL wrong?**

I recognize this is not purely an either/or scenario, and relationships that began with a Twitter exchange or series of blog comments can flourish into treasured real-world ties.

**40**    But those situations where we "meet" someone through social media, have the opportunity to interact in real life, and then develop a relationship that creates true friendship are few and far between. **And as social media gets bigger and more pervasive, this chasm becomes even more difficult to cross.** As my own networks in social media have gotten larger, I've ended up talking about my personal life less, because a large percentage of that group don't know me, or my wife, or my kids, or my town, or my interests. I don't want to bore people with the inanities of the everyday. (Facebook is the one exception, as I've always kept my personal account relatively small).

**50**    To some degree, I think this explains the popularity of Google + among people with very large followings on Twitter and/or Facebook. Google + provides a chance for a do-over, to create a new group of connections that are more carefully cultivated.

But that's just medicating the symptoms, not curing the disease. **Fundamentally, technology and our use of it isn't—as we've all hoped—bringing us closer together.** In fact, it may be driving us farther apart, as we know more and more people, but know less and less about each of them.

## Making Friends Out of Connections

60      **Maybe we should be focused less on making a lot of connections, and focused more on making a few real friends?** I'm going to try to work on this, to identify people with whom I want to develop real friendships, and make a concerted effort to do so, even if it means answering fewer tweets and blog comments from a much larger group of casual connections.

We have to take at least some of these social media spawned relationships to the next level, otherwise what's the point beyond generating clicks and newsletter subscribers?

**You think you know someone, but you don't. And that's social**
70    **media's fault. But more so, our own.**

## Close Read

What claim and counterclaim about the value of Internet contacts does the blogger make? Be sure to cite textual evidence in your response.

_____

_____

_____

1. Analyze      2. Practice      3. Perform

# Making Friends Through The Internet
**Advantages and disadvantages of meeting friends online**
by Sally Arthur

Meeting friends on the Internet can have its advantages and disadvantages. There are a number of factors to consider.

Meeting friends online can happen more quickly than it might happen offline. You can even become friends with someone who lives in a different part of the world.

You can remain anonymous on the Internet. You do not have to share information about where you live, how old you are, or any personal details about your life. Online, you can be whoever you want to be, or just be yourself. This allows people to practice their
10 social skills in an anonymous setting.

One major disadvantage of making friends online is that you do not always know if people are who they say they are. Just as it can be a good thing to be anonymous to protect your safety and personal information, anonymity can be dangerous, too. If you are dealing with someone who is not forthcoming about their identity, you don't know his or her motive for doing so.

Making friends online also may prevent people from socializing outside of the Internet. While having friends online is a good way to find people with similar interests, friends who exist only on a
20 computer screen do not provide the companionship necessary to sustain friendships. If having Internet friends comes at the cost of neglecting friends offline, the Internet becomes a disadvantage.

While there are advantages and disadvantages to meeting friends online, it is up to every individual to use discretion and be safe.

**NOTES**

## Discuss and Decide

Reviewing the advantages and disadvantages Arthur lists, do you have a sense of her bias? Explain your thinking, citing evidence from the text.

# Respond to Questions on Step 3 Sources

These questions will help you analyze the sources you've read. Use your notes and refer back to the sources to answer the questions. Your answers to these questions will help you write your essay.

**1** Is the evidence from one source more credible than the evidence from another source? When you evaluate the credibility of a source, examine the expertise of the author and/or the organization responsible for the information. Record your reasons.

| Source | Credible? | Reasons |
|---|---|---|
| **Newspaper Article** Study: The Internet Helps You Make More Friends, Be More Social | | |
| **Blog** Social Media, Pretend Friends, and the Lie of False Intimacy | | |
| **Magazine Article** Making Friends Through the Internet | | |

**2** **Prose Constructed-Response** What point about making friends online is raised in all three sources? Why is this point important to address when making an informed decision about the validity of online friendships? Support your answer with details and evidence.

_____

_____

_____

**3** **Prose Constructed-Response** Does the evidence in "Making Friends Through the Internet" support or contradict the evidence in "Study: The Internet Helps You Make More Friends, Be More Social"? Use details from the article to support your answer.

_____

_____

_____

# Part 2: Write

## Plan

Use the graphic organizer to help you outline the structure of your argumentative essay.

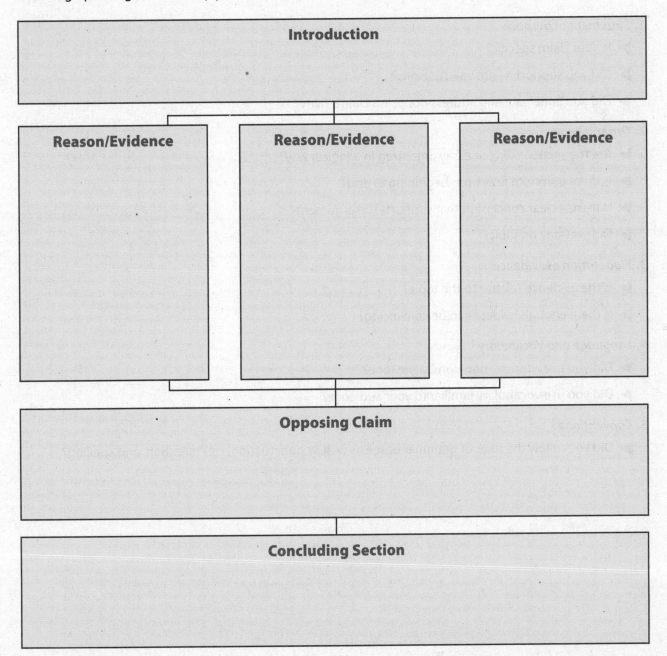

**Introduction**

**Reason/Evidence**

**Reason/Evidence**

**Reason/Evidence**

**Opposing Claim**

**Concluding Section**

# Draft

 Use your notes and completed graphic organizer to write a first draft of your argumentative essay.

# Revise and Edit

 Look back over your essay and compare it to the Evaluation Criteria. Revise your essay and edit it to correct spelling, grammar, and punctuation errors.

# Evaluation Criteria

Your teacher will be looking for:

**1. *Statement of purpose***

▶ Is your claim specific?

▶ Did you support it with valid reasons?

▶ Did you anticipate and address opposing claims fairly?

**2. *Organization***

▶ Are the sections of your essay organized in a logical way?

▶ Is there a smooth flow from beginning to end?

▶ Is there a clear conclusion that supports the argument?

▶ Did you stay on topic?

**3. *Elaboration of evidence***

▶ Is the evidence relative to the topic?

▶ Is there enough evidence to be convincing?

**4. *Language and Vocabulary***

▶ Did you use a formal, non-combative tone?

▶ Did you use vocabulary familiar to your audience?

**5. *Conventions***

▶ Did you follow the rules of grammar usage as well as punctuation, capitalization, and spelling?

# Ancient Civilizations

# Informative Essay

| STEP 1 | ANALYZE THE MODEL |
|---|---|
| | *Evaluate informative essays on Cuzco, Peru, and Machu Picchu.* |

| STEP 2 | PRACTICE THE TASK |
|---|---|
| | *Write a comparison/ contrast essay on how the Mayan and Egyptian pyramids are alike and different.* |

| STEP 3 | PERFORM THE TASK |
|---|---|
| | *Write an informative essay about the successes of the Maya, the Aztecs, and the Inca.* |

An informative essay, also called an expository essay, is a short work of nonfiction that informs and explains. Unlike fiction, nonfiction is mainly written to convey factual information, although writers of nonfiction shape information in a way that matches their own purposes. Nonfiction writing can be found in newspaper, magazine, and online articles, as well as in biographies, speeches, movie and book reviews, and true-life adventure stories.

The nonfiction topics that you will read about in this unit discuss real facts and events about ancient civilizations and structures.

**IN THIS UNIT,** you will analyze information from nonfiction articles, graphics, and data displays. You will study a variety of text structures that are frequently used in the writing of informative text. You will use these text structures to plan and write your essays.

*Exploring Peru*

## You will read:

▶ **AN INSTRUCTIONAL ARTICLE**
*Chart a Course That Works!*

## You will analyze:

▶ **TWO STUDENT MODELS**
*Cuzco, Peru*

*Machu Picchu*

# Source Materials for Step 1

Ms. Margolis' students read the article below to help them learn strategies for structuring informative essays. As you read, underline information that you find useful.

**NOTES**

# Chart a Course That Works!

You probably have already had tough writing assignments that required you to plan, research, and write an informative essay. Whether the subject is science, history, or another nonfiction topic, you should decide in advance how you will structure your essay. Don't just start somewhere and keep on writing until you have met the page requirement. Structure first! What do I mean by structure? A structure is a system in which the parts all have a function. When you write an informative essay, each part should support your message. Graphic organizers can help you plan your organizational structure.

## Main Idea and Supporting Details

The purpose of any informative essay is to give your reader more information about a topic, whether that be explaining a topic or describing a process. Use a graphic organizer like the one below to focus on your main idea and the details or descriptions to support it. Jot down your main idea or central point. Then identify the details you will use to support or explain your main idea. To keep on track, refer regularly to your graphic organizer as you write.

# Developing Your Topic

Many scientific and historical essays revolve around cause-effect relationships. Sometimes multiple factors contribute to one event. Sometimes a single event can lead to multiple outcomes. In some situations, one event triggers the next event to happen, and that causes another event to occur.

## 1. Cause-to-Effect Organization

A power outage affects people in multiple ways.

## 2. Multiple-Causes Organization

Teenage obesity is caused by a number of factors.

## 3. Chronological Order

Events happen in chronological order, which means that one event follows another. There is a sequence of events that occur in time order.

**Discuss and Decide**

What are some events that can be told in chronological order?

# Analyze Two Student Models for Step 1

Ken structured his informative essay topically, relating the main idea first, followed by its supporting details. Read his essay closely. The red side notes are comments made by his teacher, Ms. Margolis.

**Ken's Model**

```
            MAIN IDEA
      Cuzco is a unique city.
  ┌──────┬──────────┬──────────┐
History  Architecture  Festivals  Prestigious
                      & Food      Awards
```

Ken Norris
Ms. Margolis, English
March 15

# Cuzco, Peru

In southeastern Peru, nestled in the Andes at a height of 11,200 feet above sea level, is one of the world's most amazing cities. It's Cuzco, or *Qosqo* as it was called in ancient Incan times, a name which means "navel of the earth."

Perhaps the most amazing thing about Cuzco is its history. The city is said to be one of the oldest inhabited developments in the Americas. The earliest inhabitants were the Killki; their culture was dominant in the area for over a thousand years. The next important group in the area were the Incas. Their civilization began in the 12th century, and by the early 1400s the Inca Empire began to expand very quickly. Sometime around 1450, the inca (king) Pachacutec developed Cuzco into the capital of the empire. The city was designed in the shape of a puma, and two rivers were diverted with canals to prevent flooding. By 1500, Cuzco was one of the richest and most important cities in the Americas.

But then something new happened on the continent. Spanish conquistadors arrived. The Incas were involved in civil war, many fell victim to European diseases, and their warriors were no match for Spanish armored horseback cavalry. In 1533, a Spanish force of just 180 men under Francisco Pizarro took the city. Three

*good chronological account of the history of the area*

© Houghton Mifflin Harcourt Publishing Company

years later, a force of between 10,000 and 100,000 Incas tried unsuccessfully to reclaim it. Cuzco remained under Spanish rule until 1821, when Peru declared independence.

One of the results of the Spanish conquest was the remarkable mix of architecture in Cuzco. The Inca stonework and precious metals were like nothing Spaniards had ever seen. Great blocks of stone were so accurately cut that there was no need for mortar. One such block that remains as part of a wall weighs over 30 tons. The Spanish took the precious metals, including 700 gold panels from the Qorikancha temple that each weighed nearly five pounds. They destroyed the Inca's religious and political buildings, but built their own churches and palaces on the Inca foundations. The city retains its Inca layout and numerous examples of both Inca stonework and Spanish baroque architecture.

*very interesting to learn how the Spanish and Incan influences both remain in the city*

A modern visitor to Cuzco will delight in the city's festivals, its indigenous foods (such as the famed "cuy," roasted guinea pig), its temples and palaces, and its sacred history.

*Did the Spanish conquerors have an influence on these festivals?*

For these and many other reasons, Cuzco is a most amazing city. It is no wonder that it has been called the archaeological capital of the Americas, has been named to UNESCO's Cultural Heritage List, and is also a World Heritage Site.

## Discuss and Decide

Discuss at least two reasons why Cuzco is considered a World Heritage site. Cite text evidence in your discussion.

Claudia chose to use a chronological text structure for her essay. In this essay, Claudia describes the history of Machu Picchu, from its discovery to its classification as a World Heritage site. Ms. Margolis made her notes in red.

## Claudia's Model

Machu Picchu's beginnings → Hiram Bingham and Machu Picchu → Location → Machu Picchu in the present

Claudia Zhang
Ms. Margolis, English
March 15

# Machu Picchu

### Machu Picchu's Beginnings

Machu Picchu, "The Lost City of the Incas," is the site of one of the most well-known set of ruins in the world. Historians believe that Machu Picchu was constructed during the height of the Inca Empire in the 15th century. About 100 years after it was built, Machu Picchu was abandoned, though historians are not sure of the exact reason why. The Spanish had arrived in South America around this time, so some consider this a possible explanation for its abandonment. However, there is no evidence that the Spanish ever entered Machu Picchu. Some historians believe a smallpox epidemic forced the Inca to leave Machu Picchu.

*That is quite the mystery! Are there any other theories to account for its abandonment?*

Another mystery that surrounds Machu Picchu is what its purpose was. Some archaeologists believe that the city was a royal estate for Inca nobles and emperors. Other guesses have included a women's retreat, a city created solely for the coronation of kings, a prison, or a site for testing new crops. The belief that Machu Picchu might have been a religious site is supported by its geographic location, close to the mountains and other natural features that were important to the Inca.

### Hiram Bingham and Machu Picchu

Hiram Bingham, an American archaeologist, was searching for the Incan city of Vilcabamba when he arrived at Machu Picchu in

1. Analyze    2. Practice    3. Perform

the summer of 1911. Bingham and his team of explorers walked on foot and traveled on mules to journey from Cuzco to the Urubamba Valley in Peru. A farmer told them of the ruins at the top of the mountain. On July 24, led by a small group of peasants and an 11-year-old boy, Bingham first saw Machu Picchu.

*Think about including more detail in this paragraph: how long did the trip take?*

Bingham excavated artifacts from the site and brought them to Yale University. He also wrote a book called *The Lost City of the Incas* that prompted many eager tourists to travel to Peru and make the same journey Bingham had made along the Inca Trail. Machu Picchu was no longer known to just the local peasants, but had become a travel destination for the world.

In the history books, Bingham is listed as the person who made Machu Picchu known to the world, but it is believed that missionaries and other explorers had arrived at Machu Picchu in the 19th and early 20th centuries.

*I see why he wouldn't be named as the person to "discover" Machu Picchu, since it had never been lost!*

## Location

Machu Picchu is located in the mountain forests of the Peruvian Andes. Terraces, walls, and stairways peek out from the sloping mountains, creating a sight that is beautiful to the eye. The Incas used stones to hammer the larger stones together snugly, without mortar.

The site has terraced fields and a complex irrigation system that would have been useful in the different sectors of the city, including a farming zone, a royal district, a sacred area, and a residential neighborhood.

*The Inca were an advanced society. Strong facts support the theories you presented about the site's purpose.*

## Machu Picchu in the Present

In 2007, Machu Picchu was named one of the New Seven Wonders of the World. It is Peru's most visited site, as well as South America's most famous ruins. To protect the ruins and prevent mountainside erosion, the government has taken steps to ensure that tourists exercise proper care when visiting the site.

## Discuss and Decide

Why is Machu Picchu known as the "Lost City of the Incas"?

# Terminology of Informative Essays

Read each term and explanation. Then look back and analyze each student model. Find an example to complete the chart.

| Term | Explanation | Example from Student Essays |
|------|-------------|----------------------------|
| topic | The **topic** is a word or phrase that tells what the essay is about. | |
| text structure | The **text structure** is the organizational pattern of an essay. | |
| focus | The **focus** is the controlling, or overarching, idea that states the main point the writer chooses to make. | |
| supporting evidence | The **supporting evidence** is relevant quotations and concrete details that support the focus. | |
| domain-specific vocabulary | **Domain-specific vocabulary** is content-specific words that are not generally used in conversation. | |
| text features | **Text features** are design elements that help organize the text, such as headings, boldface type, italic type, bulleted or numbered lists, sidebars, and graphic aids including charts, tables, timelines, illustrations, and photographs. | |

**Prose Constructed-Reponse** Which essay provided more details to support its main idea? Support your claim by citing text evidence.

_____

_____

_____

# In what ways are the Mayan and Egyptian pyramids alike and different?

## You will read:

▶ **A MAGAZINE ARTICLE**
*The Pyramids of Giza*

▶ **DATA ANALYSIS**
*The Great Pyramid at Giza*

▶ **A TRAVEL GUIDE**
*Visiting the Mayan Pyramids*

▶ **INFOGRAPHIC**
*El Castillo Mayan Pyramid*
*The Great Pyramid at Giza*

## You will write:

▶ **A COMPARISON / CONTRAST ESSAY**
*In what ways are the Mayan and Egyptian pyramids alike and different?*

# Source Materials for Step 2

**AS YOU READ** You will be writing a comparison-and-contrast essay about the Mayan and Egyptian pyramids. Carefully study the sources in Step 2. For each text, annotate by underlining and circling information that may be useful to you when you write your essay.

## Source 1: Magazine Article

# THE PYRAMIDS OF GIZA

by Helena Gustafson

When you hear the word *pyramids,* what picture do you see in your head? More likely than not, you see three magnificent stone structures rising out of the desert sands. These are the pyramids of Giza, Egypt, famous not only for their stupendous size and dramatic shape, but also for the astonishing skill with which they were built thousands of years ago.

The pyramids at Giza

1. Analyze    2. Practice    3. Perform

Silhouettes of the three largest pyramids at Giza: Menkaura, Khafra, and Khufu

The three pyramids at Giza were designed as monumental tombs for pharaohs (kings) of Egypt, to house their bodies after death and to help them achieve eternal life in the afterworld. Each was made by and for a different pharaoh: King Khufu built the Great Pyramid (the biggest) first, around 2550 BC; King Khafra built the second pyramid around 2520 BC; King Menkaura built the third (smallest of the three and last) in about 2490 BC.

Although there are a few passageways and chambers inside each pyramid, the structures are mostly solid stone. They were designed to be permanently sealed after the bodies of the pharaohs were placed inside. Neither the inside nor the outside of the pyramid had any public function other than to memorialize the powerful king buried inside.

As impressive as they look today, the Giza pyramids were even more striking when first built. Originally, the four faces of each pyramid were covered with a smooth layer of bright white limestone blocks that would have gleamed and glittered in the sunlight. After these casing blocks fell or were stripped off hundreds of years ago, many were hauled away and used to build mosques and houses in the city of Cairo nearby.

The pyramids at Giza have been astonishing humanity for more than 4,500 years. Successive generations of travelers, invaders, and explorers have come across them and marveled: Ancient Greeks, Arab conquerors, even Napoleon.

Even in Ancient Egyptian times, the Giza pyramids were antiques. They were more than a thousand years old at the time of King Tutankhamen. The largest pyramid at Giza is the only one of the Seven Wonders of the Ancient World that remains; to this day, it is a sight that amazes all who see it.

## Discuss and Decide

If you were to write a travel brochure advertising a visit to the Giza pyramids, which facts would you highlight and why?

# Source 2: Data Analysis

| The Great Pyramid at Giza | |
|---|---|
| **Pyramid Statistics** | |
| Height | Originally 481 feet high, the pyramid; currently stands at 450 feet. It is higher than the Statue of Liberty, St. Peter's Basilica in Rome, or Big Ben in London. |
| Base | Each side is 756 feet. The construction was so accurate, there is only a 7.9-inch difference between the longest and shortest sides of the base. Almost ten football fields would fit into the base. |
| Accuracy | The blocks were shaped and placed so perfectly that even today it is not possible to squeeze a knife blade between them. |
| **How Was the Great Pyramid at Giza Built?** | |
| Skilled laborers | Some archaeologists estimate it took 4,000 skilled laborers at least 20 years. |
| Materials | The pyramid is comprised of approximately 2,300,000 limestone and granite blocks, each weighing an average of 2.5 tons, for a total weight of 5,750,000 tons. |
| Transport | Some of the stone blocks were transported by boat from quarries as far as 500 miles away. |
| Construction | Stones were hauled into place on sleds pulled by teams of at least 30 men, without the help of engines, pulleys, or even wheeled carts. |
| Simple tools | The builders had copper, bronze, wood, and stone tools—no iron or steel. The Great Pyramid was built using simple, hand-held tools such as chisels, mallets, rock pounders and polishers, and small wooden clamps. |
| Largest pieces of stone | The largest slabs of stone are above the King's Chamber, inside the Great Pyramid. They weigh about 50 tons each. |
| Ramp | Archaeologists suggest that a huge ramp was built, allowing stones to be hauled to the top. The ramp would have to be raised as the pyramid grew taller. |
| **Notable Records** | |
| Tallest man-made structure | The Great Pyramid was the tallest man-made structure for more than 3,800 years. |
| Visibility | The three pyramids at Giza are visible from space. |
| Alignment | The four sides of the Great Pyramid align almost exactly with true north, south, east, and west; without the magnetic compass, the builders probably used the stars to make their calculations. |

1. Analyze     2. Practice     3. Perform

# Source 3: Travel Guide

## ✈ Visiting the

# MaYaN PYRaMiDS

### Where can I find the Mayan pyramids?

If you want to find a Mayan pyramid, go to Central America! The Maya were a Mesoamerican civilization that arose around 1500 BC. They built most of their pyramids between the 3rd and 9th century AD, all across eastern Mexico, Belize, Guatemala, Honduras, and El Salvador.

### What do they look like?

While Mayan pyramids come in a variety of shapes and sizes, most are step pyramids;

The ruins at Chichen Itza, a city in the Yucatán built by the Mayans.

The entrance to the pyramid is at the very top, not the bottom.

the sides are not smooth but instead rise up in stages, like giant stairs. Often there are one or more actual staircases built on top of the steps, leading to a temple or sanctuary at the top.

Compared to the Egyptian pyramids at Giza, Mayan pyramids are mostly smaller, but steeper and more ornate. They were built of stone blocks held together with lime mortar. Some were covered with plaster and painted. The Maya were expert astronomers, so their pyramids were positioned and constructed to note important points in the calendar, such as the solstice and equinox.

The pyramids played an important part in the religious and community life of the people.

Looking up the terraces toward the top of the pyramid.

Mayan pyramids functioned as temples, whether or not they were also tombs of high-ranking officials. Only priests were allowed to climb the stairs to the top. There they performed religious rituals including sacrifices. The pyramids were often part of large complexes that included palaces, ball courts, plazas, and courtyards.

Sometimes a new pyramid was built on top of an old one. If you were to dig down inside a Mayan pyramid built in, say, 800 AD, you might find the ruins of one built hundreds of years earlier.

**What else do I need to know for my visit?**
Mayan civilization flourished between around 250 and 900 AD, at which point it went into a sudden and mysterious decline. Many cities and towns were abandoned and completely swallowed up by the jungle. Although the local people may have known about them—and although Spanish conquistadors had written about them—many of the most impressive Mayan archeological sites were not "rediscovered" by Europeans until 1839 and later. Even now there are Mayan pyramids hiding in the thick jungle, waiting to be "discovered" by an intrepid explorer.

Maybe that explorer will be you!

The Mayan Civilization

## Discuss and Decide

Explain at least three differences between Mayan and Egyptian pyramids, and the reason for one of these differences. Cite text evidence in your discussion.

1. Analyze    2. Practice    3. Perform

# Source 4: Infographic

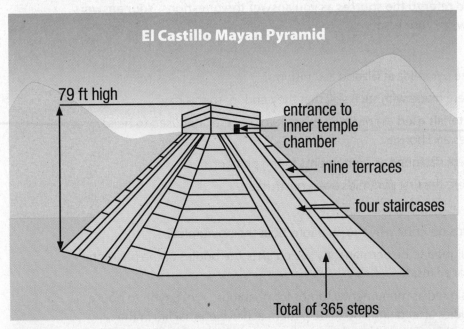

**El Castillo Mayan Pyramid**

79 ft high

entrance to inner temple chamber

nine terraces

four staircases

Total of 365 steps

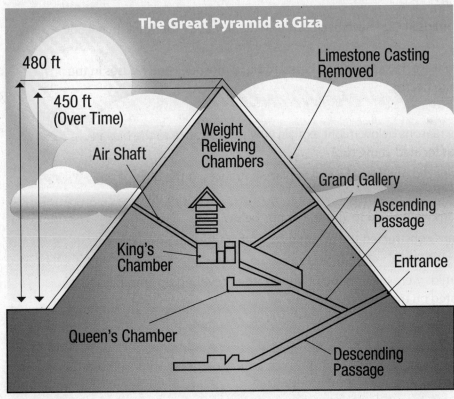

**The Great Pyramid at Giza**

480 ft

450 ft (Over Time)

Limestone Casting Removed

Weight Relieving Chambers

Air Shaft

Grand Gallery

Ascending Passage

King's Chamber

Entrance

Queen's Chamber

Descending Passage

## Discuss and Decide

What information about Egyptian pyramids does the infographic provide that the previous two sources do not?

# Respond to Questions on Step 2 Sources

**The following questions will help you think about the sources you've read. Use your notes and refer to the sources as you answer the questions. Your answers will help you write your essay.**

**1** Why are the pyramids at Giza so astonishing?

   **a.** They were made with such skill that they endure to this day.

   **b.** The materials used to construct the pyramids were later used to build mosques and houses.

   **c.** They were designed as monuments to the pharaohs.

   **d.** They were the first pyramids ever constructed.

**2** Which words describe why the pharaohs built their pyramids?

   **a.** " . . . designed to be permanently sealed after the bodies of the pharaohs were placed inside."

   **b.** " . . . designed as monumental tombs for pharaohs . . . of Egypt, to house their bodies after death and to help them achieve eternal life in the afterworld."

   **c.** "The pyramids at Giza have been astonishing humanity for more than 4,500 years."

   **d.** " . . . many were hauled away and used to build mosques and houses in the city of Cairo nearby."

**3** Which of the reasons below might explain why the entrance to the Mayan pyramids was located at the top?

   **a.** The Mayans did not have the skill to place entrances at the base of the pyramids.

   **b.** The Mayans were afraid to visit the tombs below.

   **c.** The Mayans constructed the pyramids to note important astronomical events.

   **d.** The pyramids were built on top of one another, covering up entrances that once existed on the bottom.

1. Analyze   2. Practice   3. Perform

4 Which of the following claims is *not* true?

   **a.** The pyramids at Giza were built by different pharaohs.

   **b.** The pyramids at Giza are visible from space.

   **c.** The staircases on Mayan pyramids played a role in religious rituals.

   **d.** The pyramids at Giza were less stunning when they were first built.

5 Which of the selections below best support the correct claim in Question 4?

   **a.** "Mayan pyramids functioned as temples, whether or not they were also tombs."

   **b.** "King Khufu built the Great Pyramid (the biggest) first, around 2550 BC . . ."

   **c.** "Even in Ancient Egyptian times the Giza pyramids were antiques."

   **d.** ". . . the faces of each pyramid were covered with a smooth layer of bright white limestone blocks that would have gleamed . . ."

6 **Prose Constructed-Response**  What do the graphic representations of the Mayan pyramid and the Great Pyramid at Giza help you better understand about pyramids? Explain.

_____

_____

_____

_____

7 **Prose Constructed-Response**  What is the main idea of the article "The Pyramids of Giza"? Be sure to state the main idea of the selection, as well as its supporting details. Cite text evidence in your response.

_____

_____

_____

_____

Write a comparison/contrast essay to answer the
question: In what ways are the Mayan and Egyptian
pyramids alike and different?

# Planning and Prewriting

When you write a compare-and-contrast essay, first decide what main idea your
reading brings to mind. For your essay, you should find facts that show similarities
and differences between the two types of pyramids.

 You may prefer to do your planning on your computer.

## Decide on Key Points

Summarize the key points that you will include in your essay.

| Characteristics | Mayan Pyramids | Egyptian Pyramids |
|---|---|---|
| **1. Physical Appearance** | | |
| **2. Purpose** | | |
| **3. Construction Method** | | |
| **4. Permanence** | | |

1. Analyze    2. Practice    3. Perform

# Developing Your Topic

Before you write your essay, decide how you want to arrange your ideas. You can use one of the patterns of organizing described below or come up with your own arrangement—whatever works best for your subject. Your essay will begin with an introductory paragraph and end with a concluding paragraph.

**Point-by-Point** Discuss the first point of comparison or contrast for both topics, then move on to the second point. You read across the rows of this chart.

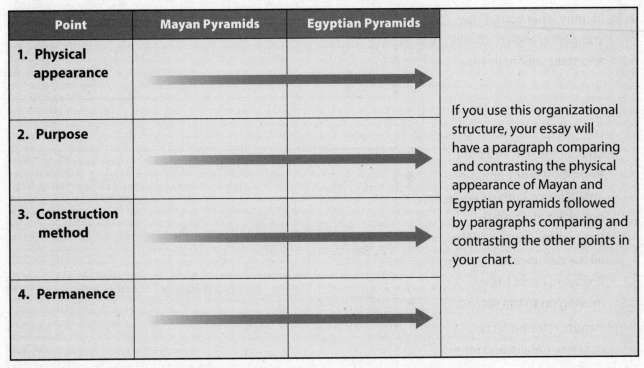

| Point | Mayan Pyramids | Egyptian Pyramids | |
|---|---|---|---|
| 1. Physical appearance | | | If you use this organizational structure, your essay will have a paragraph comparing and contrasting the physical appearance of Mayan and Egyptian pyramids followed by paragraphs comparing and contrasting the other points in your chart. |
| 2. Purpose | | | |
| 3. Construction method | | | |
| 4. Permanence | | | |

**Subject-by-Subject** Discuss all the points about one topic before moving on to the next. You read across the rows of this chart.

| Selection | Physical Appearance | Purpose | Construction Method | Permanence |
|---|---|---|---|---|
| 1. Mayan pyramids | | | | |
| 2. Egyptian pyramids | | | | |

If you use this organizational structure, your essay will have one or two paragraphs addressing all your points as they relate to Mayan pyramids, followed by one or two paragraphs addressing all your points as they relate to Egyptian pyramids.

# Finalize Your Plan

Use your responses and notes from previous pages to create a detailed plan for your essay. Fill in the chart below.

▶ Hook your audience with an interesting detail, question, or quotation.

▶ Identify what you will be comparing and contrasting and state your main idea.

▶ Choose the text structure: **Point-by-Point** Compare and contrast both subjects, one point at a time; or **Subject-by-Subject** Discuss all the points relating to the first wind event before moving on to the second.

▶ Include relevant facts, concrete details, and other evidence.

▶ Summarize the key points and restate your main idea.

▶ Include an insight that follows from and supports your main idea.

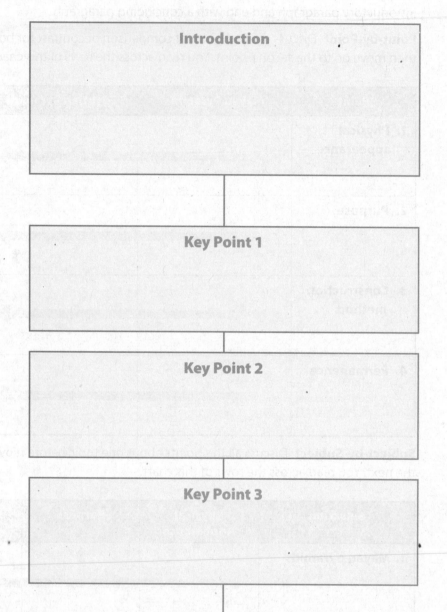

Introduction

Key Point 1

Key Point 2

Key Point 3

Conclusion

# Draft Your Essay

▶ **Your Audience:** Your teacher

▶ **Your Purpose:** Demonstrate your understanding of the specific requirements of an informative essay with a comparison/contrast text structure.

▶ **Style:** Use a formal and objective tone.

▶ **Transitions:** Use words and phrases such as *for example* or *because* to create cohesion, or flow.

# Revise

## Revision Checklist: Self Evaluation

 If you drafted your essay on the computer, you may wish to print it out so that you can more easily evaluate it.

Use the checklist below to guide your analysis.

| Ask Yourself | Tips | Revision Strategies |
|---|---|---|
| **1.** Does the introduction grab the audience's attention? | Underline sentences in the introduction that engage readers. | Add an interesting question, fact, or observation to get the reader's attention. |
| **2.** Is each point of comparison supported by textual evidence, facts, and concrete details? | Circle textual evidence. | Add textual evidence if necessary. |
| **3.** Are appropriate and varied transitions used to connect and contrast ideas? | Place a checkmark next to each transitional word or phrase. | Add transitional words or phrases where needed to clarify the relationships between ideas. |
| **4.** Does the concluding section sum up key ideas? Does it give the audience something to think about? | Double underline the summary of key points in the concluding section. Underline the insight offered to readers. | Add an overarching view of key points or a final observation about the significance of the comparison and contrast. |

# Revision Checklist: Peer Review

Exchange your essay with a classmate, or read it aloud to your partner. As you read and comment on your classmate's essay, focus on how clearly the comparison and contrast have been supported by details. Help each other identify parts of the drafts that need strengthening, reworking, or even a complete new approach.

| What To Look For | Notes for My Partner |
|---|---|
| **1.** Does the introduction grab the audience's attention? | |
| **2.** Is each point of comparison supported by textual evidence, facts, and concrete details? | |
| **3.** Are appropriate and varied transitions used to connect and contrast ideas? | |
| **4.** Does the concluding section sum up key ideas? Does it give the audience something to think about? | |

# Edit

 Edit your essay to correct spelling, grammar, and punctuation errors.

## *In what ways were the Maya, the Aztecs, and the Inca advanced for their time?*

### You will read:

▶ **THREE INFORMATIVE ARTICLES**

*Mayan Civilization*

*Aztecs*

*The Inca*

### You will write:

▶ **AN INFORMATIVE ESSAY**

*In what ways were the Maya, the Aztecs, and the Inca advanced for their time?*

# Part 1: Read Sources

## Source 1: Informative Article

# Mayan Civilization

## by Suzanne Hopkins

**AS YOU READ** *Identify key terms that you might want to use in your essay.*

**NOTES**

Long before the rise of the Inca and Aztec Empires, Mayan civilization flourished in Central America. The Maya first settled in the region as early as 1500 BC, growing maize and living in small agricultural communities. But by about AD 200, these villages were becoming cities. At its height, Mayan civilization included more than 40 cities, each with a population of 5,000 to 50,000 people. The cities had huge stone buildings, including palaces, pyramids, and temples. Each city-state was ruled by a king.

### Mayan Society

Mayan society was hierarchical, divided by both class and
10    profession. Below the king was a class of nobles; a middle class was composed of priests and commoners; at the lowest level were slaves.

The Maya were never an empire. Although the cities shared the same culture, each operated independently. They traded goods with each other, including salt, shells, cotton, corn, rubber, incense, feathers, jade, flint, obsidian, and granite were carried in huge dugout canoes along rivers and around coasts. They also fought wars, but these were on a small scale, one city against another.

### A Time of Prosperity

For many centuries, the Maya prospered. They studied the stars
and developed sophisticated and accurate calendars; practiced elaborate
20    (if gory) religious rituals and worshiped a crowded pantheon of gods and goddesses; they developed complex hieroglyphic writing that they

Image Credits: ©Digital Vision/Getty Images

© Houghton Mifflin Harcourt Publishing Company

used to record historical and religious events; they had a mathematical system based on the unit 20. Their craftsmen and artists produced fine goods made of cotton, feathers, clay, wood, and precious metals and stones, among other materials.

## Decline

Yet by AD 800, Mayan civilization was in decline. While the reasons are not fully understood, archaeologists believe that the cities had grown so large, there were not enough farmers left to supply them with food. In addition, the farmland was becoming overused, the soil
30  depleted. Food production plummeted, and famine forced people to leave the urban centers.

By AD 950, the great Mayan cities were mostly abandoned, the population dispersed into small agricultural villages. The jungle swallowed up the empty cities. The Mayan people, however, were still around when the Spanish conquistadors arrived. And they are still around today.

Though the Spanish conquered the Maya in the mid-1500s and founded cities on Mayan lands, temples and monuments remain as a testimony to the Mayans' achievements. These structures attract
40  tourists from around the world, ensuring that the Maya will never be forgotten.

## Close Read

**1.** Cite at least two reasons the Maya prospered as a civilization.

_____

_____

_____

**2.** Explain possible reasons for the decline of the Mayan empire. Cite text evidence in your response.

_____

_____

_____

# Source 2: Informative Article

# AZTECS

## by Jose Maldonado

**AS YOU READ** *Identify details that support the main idea.*

**NOTES**

Long ago, around AD 1345, a group of people in central Mexico wandered in search of a new home. These people were the Aztecs, and Aztec legend says that a prophesy led them to a group of islands on Lake Texcoco, in the Valley of Mexico. Their settlement would eventually become the great city Tenochtitlán.

As the last to arrive, the Aztec were at first ruled over by more powerful city-states in the area. But, after making alliances with some of these city-states, the Aztecs were able to defeat their overlords in 1428. Soon they began conquering other tribes across Mexico, and
10  Tenochtitlán became the center of a powerful Aztec empire.

### The Great City

At its height in 1519, the city covered about five square miles and had between 250 and 400 thousand inhabitants. It had temples, palaces, a great market, houses, and gardens. Although the city was built on a swamp, the Aztecs were able to adapt. They traveled around and through Tenochtitlán by canoe. Several raised causeways connected the island city to the mainland. They farmed special plots of land called chinampas (also known as "floating gardens")—raised areas of land built in the lake, separated by canals, where they grew maize and other crops.

20  Building cities was not the Aztecs' only accomplishment. They used picture writing to record political and religious history; they used calendars and had a mathematical system based on the number 20. They wove cotton cloth, made pottery, carved in stone and other materials, made musical instruments and elaborate costumes of feathers.

## A Hierarchical Society

Aztec society was strictly hierarchical, ruled over by a godlike emperor. Religion was an important part of everyday life, and a gory one, as they believed that human sacrifice was needed to keep the sun alive. The Aztec were harsh rulers; they demanded high tributes and

30 were constantly fighting in order to keep up a steady supply of captives to use as human sacrifice. The harsh way they ruled their empire helped to undermine them in the end.

## Decline

In 1519, Hernán Cortés and his army arrived in Tenochtitlán. When the Spanish first saw the city, they thought they must be dreaming. It was larger and more impressive than any Spanish city of the time. Vastly outnumbered, the Spanish conquistador took the Aztec emperor Montezuma II hostage and began a siege in Tenochtitlán that the Aztec could not withstand. Within three years, and with the help of the local Indian tribes who were eager to break away from Aztec rule, Cortes was

40 able to crush the Aztecs and bring about the complete collapse of their empire. The last Aztec emperor surrendered the city to Cortés in 1521, thus ending one of the most famous empires in history.

NOTES

## Close Read

**1.** Why did the Spanish think "they must be dreaming" when they saw Tenochtitlán? Cite text evidence in your response.

_____

_____

_____

**2.** Cite two reasons from the text showing how the Aztecs' harsh rule contributed to the fall of their society.

_____

_____

_____

_____

# Source 3: Informative Article

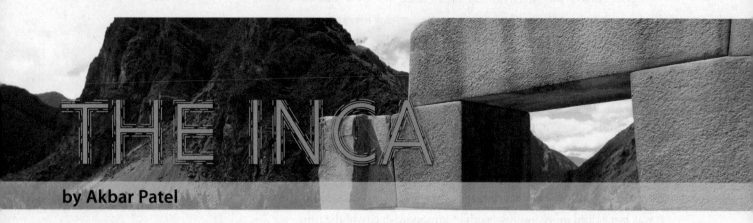

# THE INCA

## by Akbar Patel

© Houghton Mifflin Harcourt Publishing Company • Image Credits: ©Don Couch/Houghton Mifflin Harcourt

**AS YOU READ** *Identify topics addressed in this article that have also been addressed in the previous two.*

**NOTES**

Sometime in the twelfth century BC, the first Inca ruler is said to have moved his tribe to what is now Cuzco, high in the Andes. Until the fourteenth century, the Inca lived there peacefully with their neighbors. But then they began a campaign of territorial expansion that would eventually make Cuzco the capital of a vast empire.

### Establishing an Empire

Successive generations of Incan rulers worked to expand Incan territory through war and conquest. At its height, the Inca Empire stretched more than 2,000 miles along the west coast of South America and governed millions of people. The farthest reaches of the empire
10 were connected with well-constructed roads and strong rope bridges. An elaborate system of relay runners enabled messages to be carried 250 miles a day; runners made the 1,250-mile journey from Quito (a city in the far north) to Cuzco in just five days.

Incan society was hierarchical and highly centralized, with the god-like emperor at the top of the social pyramid, followed by provincial governors, local rulers and leaders, and finally the common people. The common people paid taxes and tributes and worked for the central government. The Inca did not have a writing system, but they were able to keep track of trade goods and stockpiles with a special system of
20 knotted strings called a quipu. Religion was an important part of life.

## Economy

The Inca were farmers, growing potatoes as well as other crops, often in terraces cut into the high mountainsides. They had llamas to carry loads, for wool, and for meat. They were also skilled craftsmen, building impressive cities of stone, weaving exquisite woolen cloth, and making pottery, jewelry, and many other useful and ornamental objects.

## Decline

The Spanish conquistador Francisco Pizarro arrived in Peru in 1531—a very bad time for the Inca. An emperor had died, and his two sons fought over the succession. In the ensuing war, cities were devastated, the economy was damaged, and the Inca empire was
30 divided. Pizarro used his guns, horses, and some trickery to easily defeat the Inca. New diseases brought to the Americas by the Spanish weakened the Inca as well.

Incan civilization was wiped out, but they left behind plenty of evidence of their achievements. The Incan city of Machu Picchu, for example, was never known to the Spanish invaders, but you can visit it today.

## Close Read

**1.** What was unique about the way that the Inca were able to expand their empire? Cite text evidence in your response.

_____

_____

_____

**2.** Cite evidence of the Incas' success as a civilization.

_____

_____

_____

_____

# Respond to Questions on Step 3 Sources

Read the following questions and choose the best answer for each.

**1** Which of the following claims applies only to the Aztec civilization?

   **a.** The Aztec were conquered by the Spanish.

   **b.** The Aztec were harsh rulers.

   **c.** The Aztec were skilled boatsmen.

   **d.** The Aztec were part of an empire.

**2** Which text below provides the best evidence to support the claim in Question 1?

   **a.** "They traveled around and through Tenochtitlán by canoe."

   **b.** "The last Aztec emperor surrendered the city to Cortés in 1521, thus ending one of the most famous empires in history."

   **c.** "The Maya were never an empire. Although the cities shared the same culture . . ."

   **d.** "Incan society was hierarchical and highly centralized, with the godlike emperor at the top . . ."

**3** **Prose Constructed-Response**  What factors contributed to the decline of each empire? Cite evidence from the selections in your response.

_____

_____

_____

_____

**4** **Prose Constructed-Response**  How was each society organized? Use details from the selections in your response.

_____

_____

_____

_____

1. Analyze   2. Practice   3. Perform

# Part 2: Write

**ASSIGNMENT**

You have read information about the Maya, Aztecs, and Inca. Write an informative essay that discusses why these societies were influential in both the past and the present.

## Plan

Use the graphic organizer to help you outline the structure of your informational essay.

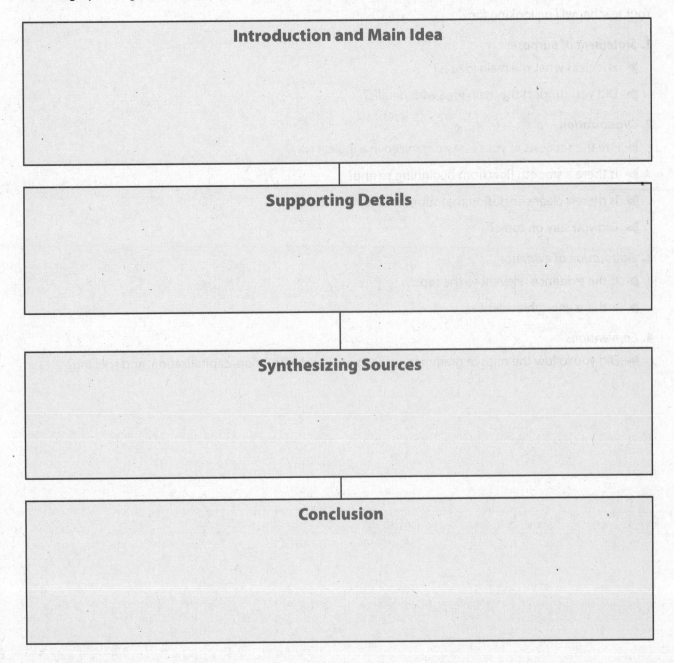

**Introduction and Main Idea**

**Supporting Details**

**Synthesizing Sources**

**Conclusion**

# Draft

 Use your notes and completed graphic organizer to write a first draft of your essay.

# Revise and Edit

 Look back over your essay and compare it to the Evaluation Criteria. Revise your essay and edit it to correct spelling, grammar, and punctuation errors.

# Evaluation Criteria

Your teacher will be looking for:

**1. *Statement of purpose***

▶ Is it clear what the main idea is?

▶ Did you support the main idea with details?

**2. *Organization***

▶ Are the sections of your essay organized in a logical way?

▶ Is there a smooth flow from beginning to end?

▶ Is there a clear conclusion that supports the main idea?

▶ Did you stay on topic?

**3. *Elaboration of evidence***

▶ Is the evidence relevant to the topic?

▶ Is there enough evidence?

**4. *Conventions***

▶ Did you follow the rules of grammar usage as well as punctuation, capitalization, and spelling?

# Changes

# Literary Analysis

STEP

**1**

## ANALYZE THE MODEL

*Evaluate an analysis of E. E. Cummings's poem "Spring is like a perhaps hand."*

STEP

**2**

## PRACTICE THE TASK

*Write an analysis of how Shakespeare uses irony in Mark Antony's speech.*

STEP

**3**

## PERFORM THE TASK

*Write a literary analysis about the ways in which Elizabeth Barrett Browning's life experiences influenced her poetry.*

Unlike nonfiction texts, literary texts—poems, stories, dramas—are not written solely to give information. They are written primarily to have an effect on the reader.

At its best, literature can cause you to react on many levels. You can be gripped by a story line or charmed by a character. The words might create a beautiful image in your mind. The mood may capture your imagination and even alter your own mood as you read.

Good literature can change readers, whether it is for the time they are reading or for a long time afterward. For example, the 19th century American philosopher and writer Henry David Thoreau championed civil disobedience as a form of protest and was inspired by the poems of Percy Bysshe Shelley. Shelley was an English Romantic poet and activist writing many decades earlier.

**IN THIS UNIT,** you will analyze another student's response to a free verse poem by E. E. Cummings. Then you will write an analysis of the use of irony in Mark Antony's speech in Shakespeare's *Julius Caesar*. Finally, you will read a sonnet by Elizabeth Barrett Browning written for Robert Browning, as well as the first two letters they wrote to each other that sparked their historic romance.

*How does the coming of
spring change us?*

## You will read:

▶ **A BIOGRAPHY**
*E.E. Cummings: The Poet and His Craft*

▶ **A POEM**
*"Spring is like a perhaps hand"*

## You will analyze:

▶ **A STUDENT MODEL**
*Winter Becomes Spring*

# Source Materials for Step 1

Mr. Winter assigned his class a poem by E.E. Cummings to read and analyze. He provided the following biography of the poet as well. The notes in the side column were written by Valerie Jones, a student in Mr. Winter's class.

## E.E. Cummings: *The Poet and His Craft*

E.E. Cummings (1894–1962) started writing poetry when he was eight years old and continued writing a poem every day until age twenty-two, when he received a degree from Harvard University. After he read some ancient classical poetry, suddenly, as he put it, "an unknown and unknowable bird started singing."

*I'll assume he's a smart guy!*

During World War I, Cummings was an ambulance driver in France. He was mistakenly arrested for treason and clapped into detention for three months. The experience was a turning point in his life. In prison, Cummings discovered his passion for freedom and personal growth. Over the next four decades he celebrated these passions.

The following quotation is from the preface to a book of Cummings's poems. The words appear here just as he wrote them.

"The poems to come are for you and for me and are not for mostpeople
—it's no use trying to pretend that mostpeople and ourselves are alike. Mostpeople have less in common with ourselves than the squarerootofminusone. You and I are human beings;mostpeople are snobs. . . ."

*Hmm . . . Why are the words bumping into each other?*

In his writing, Cummings liked to use lowercase letters, unusual word spacing (words often bump together) and his own brand of punctuation. Even though his style is new, his themes are familiar. Cummings, like lyric poets throughout the ages, celebrates the joy and wonder of life and the glory of the individual.

*AHA! Cummings likes breaking rules. I may love his poetry!*

## Discuss and Decide

With a group, discuss whether you agree with Cummings's assertion "You and I are human beings;most people are snobs." Cite text evidence in your discussion.

# Spring is like a perhaps hand

by E.E. Cummings

*a "perhaps" hand— huh?*

Spring is like a perhaps hand
(which comes carefully
out of Nowhere) arranging
a window, into which people look (while
people stare

*people looking into a window and staring out?*

arranging and changing placing
carefully there a strange
thing and a known thing here) and

changing everything carefully

*a simile*

spring is like a perhaps

*"Hand" now spelled with a capital letter.*

Hand in a window
(carefully to
and fro moving New and
Old things, while
people stare carefully
moving a perhaps

*parenthesis?*

fraction of flower here placing
an inch of air there) and

*Only 5 capital letters? Why?*

without breaking anything.

## Discuss and Decide

Review Valerie's notes in the side column. Then discuss your initial reactions to the poem with a partner. How are your reactions like or unlike Valerie's? Cite specific evidence from the text.

© Houghton Mifflin Harcourt Publishing Company • Image Credits: ©Pakhnyushcha/SuperStock

# Analyze a Student Model for Step 1

Read Valerie's literary analysis closely. The red side notes are the comments from her teacher, Mr. Winter.

Valerie Jones
Mr. Winter, English
March 24

# Winter Becomes Spring

*Good that you used these terms.*

*Important concept! Bringing it in early is helpful to the reader.*

*Your observations on the transition to spring are useful.*

In the lyric poem "Spring is like a perhaps hand," E.E. Cummings uses a simile to compare spring to a hand rearranging items in a window display. His free verse poem is full of unusual word choices and odd capitalization and punctuation. He creates an image of the gradual and uncertain morphing of winter into spring.

My experience of spring, here in the rural Northeast, is that it can be hard to know exactly when winter becomes spring. We can often see the old remnants of winter, with new spring elements peeking through. There might still be snow on the ground near where the first green shoots of daffodils are pushing up through the bare earth. Maybe spring has come, or maybe—perhaps—the wintery weather will continue.

E.E. Cummings writes about the same seasonal change in this poem. His setting seems to be a town. He describes a home or a shop with a window display and shows a hand arranging old and new items in it while passers-by stop to watch. He says that spring is like this hand. The new items in spring are things like flowers and air.

It's interesting that Cummings capitalizes only five words, *Spring, Hand, Nowhere, Old,* and *New*. These words are probably the most important ones in the poem. Spring is the topic. The words *Old* and *New* stress the change from old winter to new spring. The *Hand* is the poem's key image. *Perhaps* may be meant to caution readers that spring may not really have arrived.

Why does Cummings place *perhaps* in such an odd position in the sentence "Spring is like a perhaps hand"? The word forced me to slow down and concentrate more closely. It made me wonder whose hand was being described and why it was changing everything carefully. Maybe Cummings was saying that we can't always be certain that spring has arrived. To me, the resolution of the poem comes in the final line, "without breaking anything." Spring might come slowly, but it does come at last.

*The capitals are odd, but your explanation is interesting and plausible.*

*I really like your guess about "perhaps"! And perhaps you are right, Valerie! Very good job!*

## Discuss and Decide

With a group, decide whether or not you agree with Valerie's interpretation of the poem. Cite text evidence in your response.

© Houghton Mifflin Harcourt Publishing Company

# Terminology of Literary Analysis

Read each term and explanation. Then look back at Valerie Jones's literary analysis and find an example to complete the chart.

| Term | Explanation | Example from Valerie's Essay |
|---|---|---|
| controlling idea | The **controlling idea** is the main observation or assertion about the poem or literary work. | |
| theme | The **theme** is the underlying message about life or human nature that the writer wants the reader to understand. | |
| tone | The **tone** is the attitude the writer takes toward a subject. | |
| figurative language | **Figurative language** is language that communicates meanings beyond the literal meanings of words. Similes, metaphors, and personification are examples of figurative language. | |
| style | The **style** is the particular way in which a work of literature is written—not *what* is said but *how* it is said. | |
| voice | The **voice** is a writer's unique use of language that allows a reader to "hear" a human personality in the writer's work. | |

## How can the use of irony change our ideas?

### You will read:

▶ **A BIOGRAPHY**
*Mark Antony*

▶ **A HISTORICAL NOTE**
*Caesar's Death and Shakespeare's Play*

▶ **AN INFORMATIONAL TEXT**
*Irony in Literature*

▶ **A SPEECH**
*Mark Antony's speech from* The Tragedy of Julius Caesar, *Act III. Scene 2.*

### You will write:

▶ **A LITERARY ANALYSIS**
*How does Shakespeare use irony in Mark Antony's speech?*

# Source Materials for Step 2

**AS YOU READ** You will be writing an essay analyzing the use of irony in a famous Shakespearean speech. Carefully study the sources in Step 2. As you read, underline and circle information that may be useful to you when you write your essay.

## SOURCE 1: Biography

# MARK ANTONY

Along with Julius Caesar, Mark Antony was one of the best-known and most powerful men in Rome in the first century BC. Born in 83 BC to a family that today would be considered middle class, Antony followed in the footsteps of his father, a military commander, and gained his own fame as a cavalry officer after winning important battles for the Roman army.

In 54 BC, Antony was sent to Gaul (the ancient name for France) as an officer for Julius Caesar. The two men forged a friendship that lasted until Caesar's death. As Caesar rose to political power, he saw to it that Antony was chosen for several
10 important positions. In the Republican Civil War, Antony served as Caesar's second in command and together they defeated other powerful Roman leaders. In 44 BC, Caesar and Antony became co-consuls of Rome, the highest elected officials of the Republic.

One year earlier, the Roman Senate had declared Caesar dictator for life. However, some in the Senate feared that he would become a tyrant and began plotting to have Caesar killed. When rumors of a conspiracy against Caesar started circulating, Mark Antony rushed to alert his friend but was unable to reach him. On March 15, 44 BC, Caesar was assassinated. After his funeral oration for Caesar, Antony feared for his own life, so he fled Rome disguised as a slave. However, he soon returned to take charge of Caesar's will. When the will was made public, it revealed that Caesar had left
20 his gardens to the people of Rome and a sum of money to every Roman living in the city. Caesar's will turned the people of Rome against the assassins, since it seemed to prove that Caesar had loved his country.

## Discuss and Decide

Think about Mark Antony's relationship with Caesar. What goal might he have had in mind by giving his speech at Caesar's funeral? Cite text evidence in your discussion.

1. Analyze    2. Practice    3. Perform

© Houghton Mifflin Harcourt Publishing Company • Image Credits: ©Fernando Cortes/Shutterstock

## Source 2: Historical Note

# Caesar's Death and Shakespeare's Play

Shakespeare's play *Julius Caesar* is based on the historical events of 44 BC surrounding the death of Julius Caesar. Caesar, dictator of Rome, had made many enemies during his ascent to power. He was assassinated on March 15 by a group of senators including Brutus, a one-time supporter and friend of Caesar who nonetheless was convinced that the dictator's arrogance and power needed to be stopped.

In the play, Caesar's close friend Mark Antony, in danger himself from the assassins, wants to shift public opinion of Caesar by speaking at his funeral. Antony convinces Brutus that the assassins have nothing to fear from him, 10 so Brutus grants him permission to speak, with four conditions:

- Brutus would speak first.
- Mark Antony would speak immediately afterwards.
- Antony would not blame the conspirators.
- Antony would admit that he spoke with the conspirators' permission.

Brutus does speak first to the people of Rome and explains why he took part in the killing of Caesar: "Not that I loved Caesar less, but that I loved Rome more." Brutus presents himself as "an honourable man" and Caesar as an ambitious leader who would have enslaved the Romans. Then Antony enters with Caesar's body, and begins to speak, using Brutus's own words to sway 20 public opinion against the conspirators.

## Discuss and Decide

Think about what the assassins have done. Why might Mark Antony believe his life is in danger? Cite text evidence in your discussion.

© Houghton Mifflin Harcourt Publishing Company • Image Credits: © Comstock/Getty Images

**What Is . . .**

# Irony in Literature

### by Erica Duvall

Irony is a discrepancy or contradiction between what is said and what is meant, or between what happens and what is expected to happen. There are three main kinds of irony in literature.

**Situational irony:** A team wins the crucial basketball game only to see its leading player injured in a car accident. Someone qualifies for a competition just before the competition is canceled for lack of funds. A character tries to avoid a threat by changing his or her actions and encounters another threat instead. A person who rarely does well ends up experiencing a sudden triumph over adversity. These famous lines from Coleridge's poem, "The Rime of the Ancient Mariner" contain a great

10 example: "Water, water, every where, / Nor any drop to drink." Because situational irony is unexpected, it generally serves to shock readers rather than to create the tension of anticipation.

**Dramatic** (or tragic) **irony:** A character's words or actions convey something that is understood by readers (or the audience in the case of a play) but not by the character. This may be because the audience or readers are aware of an earlier event that the character has not witnessed or heard about. An author or playwright might use dramatic irony to increase tension, allowing the readers or audience to foresee danger that the character cannot anticipate. In *The Tragedy of Romeo and Juliet*, the audience knows Juliet drank a sleeping potion, but Romeo thinks she's dead, leading to his own

20 demise. The tension within the play builds with this realization.

**Verbal irony:** Someone says something that means one thing but is intended to mean the opposite. Sometimes a character uses irony to deliver a veiled insult while seeming to praise the person being insulted. In *The Tragedy of Julius Caesar*, each time Mark Antony repeats, "Brutus is an honourable man," we begin to wonder if, in fact, he is. Irony may be humorous or bitter, and it may or may not be obvious to its intended target. A character may use irony from a number of motives, including malice, anger, or merely the desire to be witty.

# Source 4: Speech

*from* **The Tragedy of Julius Caesar**, Act III. Scene 2. *by* **William Shakespeare**

**After Brutus speaks to the Roman people, Mark Antony enters with Caesar's body and begins to speak.**

NOTES

Friends, Romans, countrymen, lend me your ears;
I come to bury Caesar, not to praise him.
The evil that men do lives after them;
The good is oft interred with their bones;
5  So let it be with Caesar. The noble Brutus
Hath told you Caesar was ambitious:
If it were so, it was a grievous fault,
And grievously hath Caesar answer'd it.
Here, under leave of Brutus and the rest,—
10  For Brutus is an honourable man;
So are they all, all honourable men—
Come I to speak in Caesar's funeral.
He was my friend, faithful and just to me:
But Brutus says he was ambitious;
15  And Brutus is an honourable man.
He hath brought many captives home to Rome,
Whose ransoms did the general coffers fill:
Did this in Caesar seem ambitious?
When that the poor have cried, Caesar hath wept:
20  Ambition should be made of sterner stuff:
Yet Brutus says he was ambitious;
And Brutus is an honourable man.
You all did see that on the Lupercal°
I thrice presented him a kingly crown,
25  Which he did thrice refuse: was this ambition?
Yet Brutus says he was ambitious;
And, sure, he is an honourable man.
I speak not to disprove what Brutus spoke,
But here I am to speak what I do know.
30  You all did love him once, not without cause:
What cause withholds you then, to mourn for him?
O judgment! thou art fled to brutish beasts,
And men have lost their reason. Bear with me;
My heart is in the coffin there with Caesar,
35  And I must pause till it come back to me.

---

23. **Lupercal:** a festival honoring Pan

## Discuss and Decide

Does Antony follow through with his opening statement? Cite text evidence.

# Respond to Questions on Step 2 Sources

These questions will help you analyze the sources you've read. Use your notes and refer back to the sources in order to answer the questions. Your answers will help you write your essay.

**1** Why does Antony use Caesar's will to persuade the people that Caesar was not a tyrant?

   **a.** He wants the crowd to murder the conspirators.

   **b.** He wants the people to realize that Brutus wants to gain power.

   **c.** He wants the crowd to know that Brutus was jealous of Caesar.

   **d.** He wants the people of Rome to turn against the conspirators.

**2** Antony says "Brutus is an "honourable" man." Why does he repeatedly use this phrase? Antony wants to—

   **a.** convince the crowd that Brutus murdered Caesar.

   **b.** show that Brutus is actually dishonorable.

   **c.** prove that he is a better leader than Brutus.

   **d.** explain to the crowd why Brutus is admirable.

**3** Which best summarizes what Antony is trying to do in his speech? Antony is trying to—

   **a.** get Brutus and the other conspirators to admit they are murderers.

   **b.** teach the crowd about Caesar's life.

   **c.** make the crowd see that Caesar was not a tyrant.

   **d.** protect Brutus and the other conspirators.

**4** Select the three pieces of evidence from Mark Antony's speech that best support your answer to Question 1.

   **a.** "Friends, Romans, countrymen, lend me your ears" (line 1)

   **b.** ". . . The noble Brutus / Hath told you Caesar was ambitious" (lines 5–6)

   **c.** "Here, under leave of Brutus and the rest,—" (line 9)

   **d.** "When that the poor have cried, Caesar hath wept" (line 19)

   **e.** "I thrice presented him a kingly crown, / Which he did thrice refuse: was this ambition?" (lines 24–25)

   **f.** "I speak not to disprove what Brutus spoke" (line 28)

   **g.** "But here I am to speak what I do know." (line 29)

   **h.** "You all did love him once, not without cause" (line 30)

1. Analyze   2. Practice   3. Perform

**5** **Prose Constructed-Response** In what way was Mark Antony a loyal friend to Caesar? Cite evidence from his biography in your answer.

_____

_____

_____

_____

**6** **Prose Constructed-Response** Why do you think Brutus put so many conditions on Antony's speech? What do you think Brutus is afraid of? Cite evidence from Source 2.

_____

_____

_____

_____

_____

**7** **Prose Constructed-Response** Given the circumstances that surround the speech, why is irony a key tool for Antony to be able to safely achieve his goal? What kind of irony does he use?

_____

_____

_____

_____

_____

**Write a literary analysis that answers the question: How does Shakespeare use irony in Mark Antony's speech?**

# Planning and Prewriting

## Analyze the Sources

You have read a variety of texts that helped you understand the context of Mark Antony's speech. Think about how this information helped you understand Mark Antony's intentions. In the chart below, cite a fact or detail from each source that adds to the irony in his speech.

| Source | Fact or detail | How does this add to the irony of his speech? |
|---|---|---|
| **Biography** Mark Antony | | |
| **Historical Note** Caesar's Death and Shakespeare's Play | | |
| **Informational Text** Irony in Literature | | |

# Write Your Main Idea

Review your notes. In his speech, Mark Antony uses irony to express his most important ideas. Explain the use of irony in the lines below. Then state the main idea of the speech.

" . . . The noble Brutus
Hath told you Caesar was ambitious:
If it were so, it was a grievous fault,
And grievously hath Caesar answer'd it.
Here, under leave of Brutus and the rest,—
 For Brutus is an honourable man;
So are they all, all honourable men—" (lines 5–11)

_____

_____

"But Brutus says he was ambitious;
And Brutus is an honourable man.
He hath brought many captives home to Rome,
Whose ransoms did the general coffers fill:
Did this in Caesar seem ambitious?
When that the poor have cried, Caesar hath wept:
Ambition should be made of sterner stuff:
Yet Brutus says he was ambitious;
And Brutus is an honourable man." (lines 14–22)

_____

_____

"I thrice presented him a kingly crown,
Which he did thrice refuse: was this ambition?
Yet Brutus says he was ambitious;
And, sure, he is an honourable man." (lines 24–27)

_____

_____

| Main Idea |
| --- |
|  |
|  |
|  |

# Finalize Your Plan

Organize your key points in an order that makes sense for the analysis. You can address them in order of importance or in the order in which they appear.

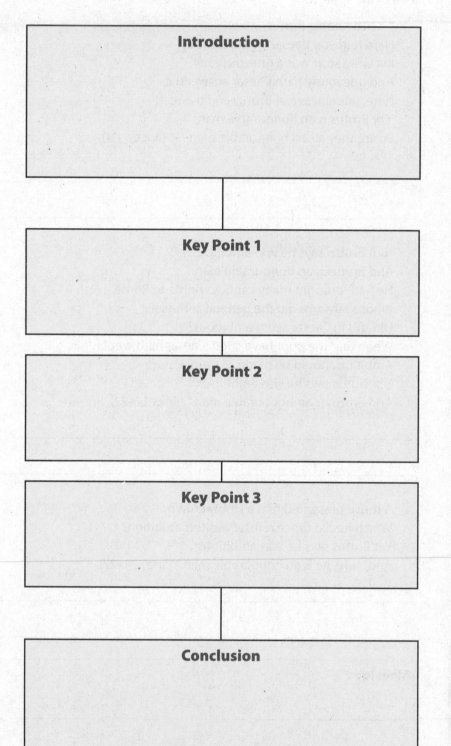

▶ Begin with a captivating comment, observation, or question about the reading.

▶ Provide necessary or interesting background information.

▶ Include your main idea.

**Introduction**

▶ State your first key point with support and elaboration.

▶ Develop a separate paragraph for each of your key points, using effective transitions between each one.

▶ Elaborate by explaining how each detail connects to each key point.

**Key Point 1**

**Key Point 2**

**Key Point 3**

▶ Restate your main idea using different words.

▶ Leave your readers with an intriguing thought.

**Conclusion**

1. Analyze    2. Practice    3. Perform

# Draft Your Essay

As you write, think about:

▶ **Audience:** Your teacher

▶ **Purpose:** Demonstrate your understanding of the specific requirements of a literary analysis.

▶ **Style:** Use a formal and objective tone.

▶ **Transitions:** Use words or phrases, such as *furthermore* or *in addition* to create cohesion, or flow.

# Revise

## Revision Checklist: Self Evaluation

Use the checklist below to guide your analysis.

 If you drafted your essay on the computer, you may wish to print it out so that you can more easily evaluate it.

| Ask Yourself | Tips | Revision Strategies |
|---|---|---|
| **1.** Does the introduction capture the audience's attention? | Underline the opening question or comment. | Add a question, observation, quote, or background information. |
| **2.** Is the controlling idea clearly stated? | Put parentheses around the controlling idea. | Rewrite your controlling idea so that it is clearly stated. |
| **3.** Are points presented in order of importance with clear and varied transitions between related ideas? | Label each paragraph with a plus, check, or minus to rate the importance of its point. Circle the transitions that link the points. | Rearrange body paragraphs to present points in order of importance. Add varied transitions to connect ideas as needed. |
| **4.** Is each point illustrated with relevant textual evidence? | Place a star next to each quotation or detail from the text. | Have at least one piece of supporting evidence for each idea. |
| **5.** Is there elaboration for each supporting detail? | Put an A next to each key point, a B next to text-evidence details, and a C next to elaboration. | Add more sentences that quote, summarize, or paraphrase. |
| **6.** Does the concluding section summarize the writer's ideas and provide an insight into the author's use of irony? | Place a check mark above the restatement of the writer's ideas and circle the concluding insight. | Add a summary of main points. Include an insight on the author's use of irony. |

# Revision Checklist: Peer Review

Exchange your essay with a classmate, or read it aloud to your partner. As you read and comment on your classmate's essay, focus on logic, organization, and evidence—not on whether you agree with the author's claim. Help each other identify parts of the drafts that need strengthening, reworking, or a new approach.

| What To Look For | Notes for My Partner |
|---|---|
| 1. Does the introduction capture the audience's attention? | |
| 2. Is the controlling idea clearly stated? | |
| 3. Are points presented in order of importance with clear and varied transitions between related ideas? | |
| 4. Is each point illustrated with relevant textual evidence? | |
| 5. Is there elaboration for each supporting detail? | |
| 6. Does the concluding section summarize the writer's ideas and provide an insight into the effect of the author's use of irony? | |

# Edit

 Edit your essay to correct spelling, grammar, and punctuation errors.

1. Analyze    2. Practice    3. Perform

*How do our life experiences change us?*

## You will read:

▶ **A BIOGRAPHY**
*The Life of Elizabeth Barrett Browning*

▶ **A HISTORICAL ESSAY**
*The Browning Letters*

▶ **A POEM**
*"Sonnet 43"*

▶ **TWO LETTERS**
*The Letters of Robert Browning and Elizabeth Barrett Barrett*

## You will write:

▶ **A LITERARY ANALYSIS**
*How did Elizabeth Barrett Browning's life experiences influence her poetry?*

### Source 1: Biography

The Life of
# Elizabeth Barrett Browning

by Alicia Kim

Born in 1806 in Durham, England, Elizabeth Barrett Browning was an English poet who gained enormous fame during her lifetime. The oldest of twelve children, she was born into great wealth, her father having made most of his fortune from sugar plantations that he owned in Jamaica. By all accounts, Elizabeth lived a privileged childhood, riding her pony around the grounds of her family's estate and visiting the local neighbors. Educated at home, she was something of a child prodigy. She writes that at age six she was reading novels. At age ten she was studying Greek, writing

10 her own epic poem in the Greek style two years later.

While living with her father in London, Elizabeth published her first book of mature poetry which gained her some fame. During these years in London, however, her ill-health (the exact cause of which is unknown) worsened, forcing her to spend a year on the coast with her favorite brother, Edward, who tragically drowned a year later. Distraught over her brother's death, Elizabeth returned home, becoming an invalid and a recluse, spending the next five years in her bedroom and seeing few people in her father's home on Wimpole Street.

20 Elizabeth continued to write, and in 1844 published a volume of poetry with the simple title of *Poems*. This book made her one of the most popular writers in England, and it gained the attention of the renowned poet Robert Browning, whose work she had praised in one of her poems. After reading these poems, Browning wrote to her saying, "I LOVE your verses with all my heart, dear Miss Barrett," and so begins one of the greatest love stories in literary history.

© Houghton Mifflin Harcourt Publishing Company • Image Credits: ©MarinaMariya/SuperStock

1. Analyze    2. Practice    3. Perform

As their correspondence continued, the couple exchanged nearly 600 letters, falling in love and marrying secretly on September 12, 1846. Although most of her family accepted the marriage, Elizabeth's
30  tyrannical father disowned her, refusing to open her letters or see her.

Out of the romantic courtship between Elizabeth Barrett and Robert Browning came an outpouring of love, which Elizabeth transformed into poetry. Giving a small packet of these sonnets to Robert, which she had written to him in secret before their marriage, her husband decided to publish them, saying that he could not keep these poems to himself, for they were "the finest sonnets written in the English language since Shakespeare's." In 1850 the poems appeared as *Sonnets from the Portuguese* and included Elizabeth's
40  most famous love poem to Robert, *Sonnet 43*, beginning, "How do I love thee? Let me count the ways."

Moving to Italy after their marriage, the Brownings and their son spent many happy years there, until Elizabeth passed away, dying in Robert's arms on June 29, 1861. Of their profound love and poetry, their friend and literary critic Frederic Kenyon wrote: ". . . no modern English poet has written of love with such genius, such beauty, and such sincerity, as the two who gave the most beautiful example of it in their own lives."

## Discuss and Decide

With a small group, discuss how Elizabeth Barrett Browning's life and experiences provide a context for her work. Cite text evidence in your discussion.

## Source 2: Historical Essay

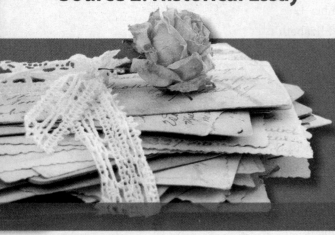

# The Browning Letters

by Gregory Evans

**AS YOU READ** *Pay close attention to the details describing the love letters written and received by the Victorian poets Robert Browning and Elizabeth Barrett Browning. Pay special attention to the historical context in which they were written.*

**NOTES**

No story of the great Victorian poets Elizabeth Barrett Browning (1806–1861) and Robert Browning (1812–1889) could be told without providing a close reading of their love letters to each other, 574 letters in all, written between January 10, 1845, and September 18, 1846. Beginning with a letter addressed to "dear Miss Barrett" and ending with Elizabeth's note to Robert as they arranged to leave England and travel to Italy a week after their marriage, the love letters of Robert and Elizabeth Barrett Browning are among the most famous in literary history, providing meaningful insights into their lives,
10 love, thoughts, feelings, experiences, and poetry.

After reading her poems for the first time, Robert Browning begins the correspondence with the line: "I LOVE your verses with all my heart, dear Miss Barrett," describing the poems as "fresh strange music," and transferring his love for her poetry into love for her before the end of the letter: "I do, as I say, love these books with all my heart—and I love you too." With that first meeting of their hearts and minds, a love affair blossoms between them. As their correspondence deepens over the course of twenty months, Elizabeth tells an acquaintance that they "are growing to be the truest of
20 friends." Yet by January 10, 1846, exactly one year after Robert's first letter, the friendship that Elizabeth has felt for him has clearly turned to love.

1. Analyze    2. Practice    3. Perform

Elizabeth writes:

> Do you know, when you have told me to think of you, I
> have been feeling ashamed of thinking of you so much,
> of thinking of only you—which is too much
> perhaps. . . . Shall I tell you? It seems to me, to myself,
> that no man was ever before to any woman what you
> are to me. . . .

30 The rest, as they say, is history, as the most romantic literary
couple of the Victorian era falls in love through their letters and
secretly marries on September 12, 1846.

Of course, the Browning letters are only one of the series of love
letters that have survived the centuries. Love letters written by Henry
VIII to Anne Boleyn, by the poet John Keats to his beloved Fanny
Brawne, by Abigail Adams to her husband John Adams are other
notable examples. Despite the different people writing them, all these
love letters have the same purpose—to sweep the recipient of the
letter off his or her feet by a frank, even poetic, display of feelings.

40 Yet the fact that the Browning letters were written by two literary
giants attests to the letters' uniqueness. Perhaps only poets can
write of love in this way, using metaphors and symbols, making the
Browning letters unparalleled for their beauty, sincerity, and deeply
poetic display of emotion.

NOTES

## Close Read

Summarize the article you have just read. How did Elizabeth Barrett and
Robert Browning fall in love? Cite text evidence in your response.

_____

_____

_____

_____

_____

# Sonnet 43

## by Elizabeth Barrett Browning

**AS YOU READ** *Focus on the form of this sonnet, a 14-line poem with a definite rhyme scheme and meter. Record comments or questions about the text in the side margin.*

**NOTES**

How do I love thee? Let me count the ways.

I love thee to the depth and breadth and height

My soul can reach, when feeling out of sight

For the ends of Being and ideal Grace.

5    I love thee to the level of everyday's

Most quiet need, by sun and candlelight.

I love thee freely, as men strive for Right;

I love thee purely, as they turn from Praise.

I love thee with passion put to use

10    In my old griefs, and with my childhood's faith.

I love thee with a love I seemed to lose

With my lost saints,—I love thee with the breath,

Smiles, tears, of all my life!—and, if God choose,

I shall but love thee better after death.

## Close Read

Reread the last six lines of the poem. How is the poet comparing the intensity of love she feels for Robert Browning with the intensity of love she had experienced earlier in her life? Cite text evidence in your response.

_____

_____

# THE LETTERS OF
# *Robert Browning* AND
# *Elizabeth Barrett Barrett*

## *R.B. to E.B.B.*

**New Cross, Hatcham, Surrey.**
**[Post-mark, January 10, 1845.]**

*I* LOVE your verses with all my heart, dear Miss Barrett,—and this is no off-hand complimentary letter that I shall write,—whatever else, no prompt matter-of-course recognition of your genius, and there a graceful and natural end of the thing. Since the day last week when I first read your poems, I quite laugh to remember how I have been turning and turning again in my mind what I should be able to tell you of their effect upon me, for in the first flush of delight I thought I would this once get out of my habit of purely passive enjoyment, when I do really enjoy, and thoroughly

10 justify my admiration—perhaps even, as a loyal fellow-craftsman should, try and find fault and do you some little good to be proud of hereafter!—but nothing comes of it all—so into me has it gone, and part of me has it become, this great living poetry of yours, not a flower of which but took root and grew. Oh, how different that is from lying to be dried and pressed flat, and prized highly, and put in a book with a proper account at top and bottom, and shut up and put away . . . and the book called a 'Flora,' besides! After all, I need not give up the thought of doing that, too, in time; because even now, talking with whoever is worthy, I can give a reason for my faith

20 in one and another excellence, the fresh strange music, the affluent language, the exquisite pathos and true new brave thought; but in this addressing myself to you—your own self, and for the first time, my feeling rises altogether. I do, as I say, love these books with all my heart—and I love you too. Do you know I was once not very far

© Houghton Mifflin Harcourt Publishing Company • Image Credits: ©V/SuperStock

**AS YOU READ** *As you read these letters, note passages or details that you find especially powerful.*

**NOTES**

from seeing—really seeing you? Mr. Kenyon said to me one morning 'Would you like to see Miss Barrett?' then he went to announce me,—then he returned . . . you were too unwell, and now it is years ago, and I feel as at some untoward passage in my travels, as if I had been close, so close, to some world's-wonder in chapel or crypt, only
30 a screen to push and I might have entered, but there was some slight, so it now seems, slight and just sufficient bar to admission, and the half-opened door shut, and I went home my thousands of miles, and the sight was never to be?

Well, these Poems were to be, and this true thankful joy and pride with which I feel myself,

Yours ever faithfully,
ROBERT BROWNING.

# E.B.B. to R.B.

**50 Wimpole Street: Jan. 11, 1845.**

*I* thank you, dear Mr. Browning, from the bottom of my heart. You meant to give me pleasure by your letter—and even if the object had not been answered, I ought still to thank you. But it is thoroughly answered. Such a letter from such a hand! Sympathy is dear—very dear to me: but the sympathy of a poet, and of such a poet, is the quintessence of sympathy to me! Will you take back my gratitude for it?—agreeing, too, that of all the commerce done in the world, from Tyre to Carthage, the exchange of sympathy for gratitude is the most princely thing! . . .

10      Is it indeed true that I was so near to the pleasure and honour of making your acquaintance? and can it be true that you look back upon the lost opportunity with any regret? *But*—you know—if you had entered the 'crypt,' you might have caught cold, or been tired to death, and *wished* yourself 'a thousand miles off;' which would have been worse than travelling them. It is not my interest, however,

to put such thoughts in your head about its being 'all for the best'; and I would rather hope (as I do) that what I lost by one chance I may recover by some future one. Winters shut me up as they do dormouse's eyes; in the spring, *we shall see*: and I am so much better
20 that I seem turning round to the outward world again. And in the meantime I have learnt to know your voice, not merely from the poetry but from the kindness in it. Mr. Kenyon often speaks of you— dear Mr. Kenyon!—who most unspeakably, or only speakably with tears in my eyes,—has been my friend and helper, and my book's friend and helper! critic and sympathiser, true friend of all hours! You know him well enough, I think, to understand that I must be grateful to him.

I am writing too much,—and notwithstanding that I am writing too much, I will write of one thing more. I will say that I am your
30 debtor, not only for this cordial letter and for all the pleasure which came with it, but in other ways, and those the highest: and I will say that while I live to follow this divine art of poetry, in proportion to my love for it and my devotion to it, I must be a devout admirer and student of your works. This is in my heart to say to you—and I say it.

And, for the rest, I am proud to remain

Your obliged and faithful
ELIZABETH B. BARRETT.

## Discuss and Decide

With a small group, discuss the content and tone of each letter. In what ways are they similar? Cite text evidence in your discussion.

# Respond to Questions on Step 3 Sources

These questions will help you think about the essays, the poem, and the letters you have read. Use your notes and refer to the sources in order to answer the questions. Your answers will help you write your essay.

**1** **Prose Constructed-Response** What comparisons about the poet's love for Robert Browning and her religious and political beliefs does she make in the first eight lines of the sonnet? Cite specific evidence from the text.

_____

_____

_____

_____

**2** **Prose Constructed-Response** What comparisons does the poet make in the last six lines of the poem?

_____

_____

_____

_____

**3** **Prose Constructed-Response** How does the essay about the Browning letters help you place the two letters you have read in both a historical and a personal context?

_____

_____

_____

_____

_____

# Part 2: Write

## Plan

Use the graphic organizer to help you outline the structure of your literary analysis.

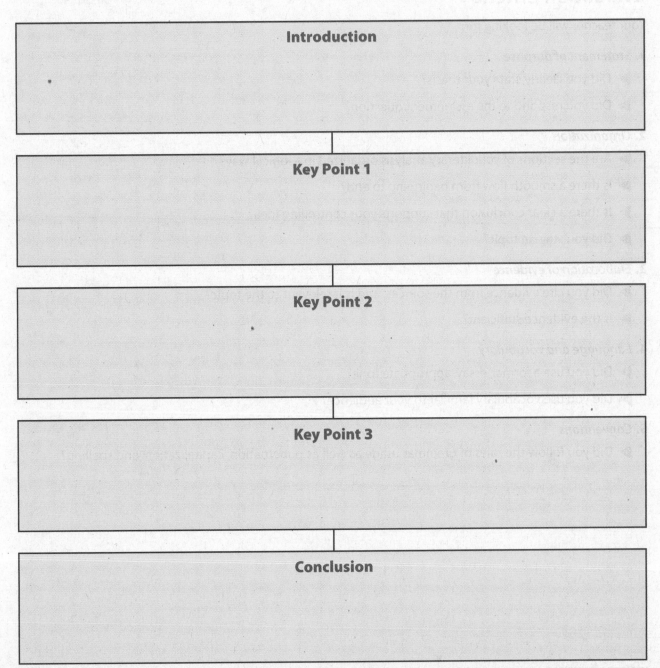

**Introduction**

**Key Point 1**

**Key Point 2**

**Key Point 3**

**Conclusion**

## Draft

 Use your notes and completed graphic organizer to write a first draft of your literary analysis.

## Revise and Edit

 Look back over your essay and compare it to the Evaluation Criteria. Revise your literary analysis and edit it to correct spelling, grammar, and punctuation errors.

## Evaluation Criteria

Your teacher will be looking for:

**1. Statement of purpose**

▶ Did you clearly state your thesis?

▶ Did you respond to the assignment question?

**2. Organization**

▶ Are the sections of your literary analysis organized in a logical way?

▶ Is there a smooth flow from beginning to end?

▶ Is there a clear conclusion that supports your controlling idea?

▶ Did you stay on topic?

**3. Elaboration of evidence**

▶ Did you cite evidence from the sources, and is it relevant to the topic?

▶ Is the evidence sufficient?

**4. Language and vocabulary**

▶ Did you use a formal, essay-appropriate tone?

▶ Did you use vocabulary familiar to your audience?

**5. Conventions**

▶ Did you follow the rules of grammar usage as well as punctuation, capitalization, and spelling?

# On Your Own

**TASK 1** RESEARCH SIMULATION
*Argumentative Essay*

**TASK 2** RESEARCH SIMULATION
*Informative Essay*

**TASK 3** *Literary Analysis*

# TASK 1

## RESEARCH SIMULATION

# *Argumentative Essay*

There is a debate in your community about whether citizens should be able to own wild animals, sometimes called exotic animals. You have decided to write a letter to the editor about this issue. Your letter will take the form of an argumentative essay.

First you will review two articles about ownership of exotic animals. After you have reviewed these sources, you will answer some questions about them. You should first skim the sources and the questions and then go back and read them carefully.

In Part 2, you will write an argumentative essay about whether you agree or disagree that it is okay for people to own exotic animals as pets.

# Time Management: Argumentative Task

There are two parts to most formal writing tests. Both parts of the tests are timed, so it's important to use your limited time wisely.

## Part 1: Read Sources and Answer Questions

### Preview the Assignment

**35 minutes**

You will have 35 minutes to read two sources about private citizens keeping exotic animals as pets. You will also answer questions about the texts.

*35 minutes! That's not much time.*

*Preview the questions. This will help you know which information you'll need to find as you read.*

### How Many?

How many pages of reading?

→ How many multiple-choice questions?

→ How many prose constructed-response questions?

### How do you plan to use the 35 minutes?

*Underline, circle, and take notes as you read. You probably won't have time to reread.*

*This is a lot to do in a short time.*

Estimated time to read:

Source #1: "Do You Really Want a Baby Tiger?"                    _____ minutes

Source #2: "REXANO Proves Politicians and Lobbyists..."          _____ minutes

Estimated time to answer questions?                               _____ minutes

**Total**                                                        **35**   **minutes**

### Any concerns?

_____

_____

_____

# Part 2: Write the Essay

**85**

How much time do you have? Pay attention to the clock!

**Plan and Write an Argumentative Essay**

85 minutes

You will have 85 minutes to plan, write, revise, and edit your essay.

**Your Plan**

Before you start to write, decide on your precise claim. Then think about the evidence you will use to support your claim.

**How do you plan to use the 85 minutes?**

Estimated time for planning the essay? ____ minutes

Estimated time for writing? ____ minutes

Be sure to leave enough time for this step.

Estimated time for editing? ____ minutes

Estimated time for checking spelling, grammar, and punctuation? ____ minutes

**Total**          **85**   **minutes**

**Notes:**

_____

_____

_____

_____

Reread your essay, making sure that the points are clear. Check that there are no spelling or punctuation mistakes.

# ▶ Your Task

> You have decided to write a letter to the editor about whether people should be able to have exotic pets. In researching the topic, you have identified two sources you will use in planning your argumentative essay.

After you have reviewed the sources, you must answer some questions about them. Briefly skim the sources and questions that follow. Then, go back and read the sources carefully so you will have the information you will need to answer the questions. Take notes on the sources as you read. You may refer back to your notes at any time during Part 1 or Part 2 of the performance task.

# ▶ Part 1 (35 minutes)

You will now read the sources. After carefully reading the sources, use the rest of the time in Part 1 to answer the three questions about them. Though your answers to these questions will help you think about what you have read and plan your essay, they will also be scored as part of the test.

© Houghton Mifflin Harcourt Publishing Company

## SOURCE #1:
# Do You Really Want a
# Baby Tiger?

*Second thoughts about owning an exotic pet*

**by Mia Lewis**

You know the story: Jenny wants a puppy, but her parents are reluctant to take the plunge. They remind her of the responsibilities that go along with pet ownership: She'll have to take it for a walk, everyday, no matter what; it'll grow up from the cute puppy it is now to a gnarly old dog; there will be messes to clean up, food to buy, and trips to the vet. Jenny says she doesn't mind any of that, and soon Fido is welcomed into the family fold. In no time at all the parents love Fido just as much as Jenny does, and Fido loves them all back. It is a story with a happy ending.

10     But what if Jenny tried to persuade her parents to buy her a fuzzy lion cub she saw advertised, or a baby chimpanzee? If they had any sense, Jenny's parents would tell her "No way" and stick to their guns. Owning an exotic pet is expensive, time consuming, and a huge responsibility. And of course, it can be dangerous. Owning a wild animal is arguably cruel to the animal in a way that owning a domestic animal isn't. Given all these considerations, it's remarkable how many people across the United States decide to become owners of exotic pets.

    For some, the allure of owning an exotic pet trumps any
20    drawbacks. After all, it's not your average Joe who owns a python, or a puff adder! A house with a monkey or lion cub in the backyard is going to stand out in the neighborhood. No one will deny that owning an exotic pet is daring and different. But many experts argue that the negatives strongly outweigh the benefits. Here's a look at some of the reasons why owning an exotic animal as a pet is NOT such a good idea.

    **They all grow up.** A cute puppy grows up to be a dog—bigger, but not dangerously so. A lion cub, on the other hand, inevitably turns into, well, a lion. Most people who own exotic pets find them
30    irresistible—and manageable—when they are small. But an adorable cub becomes a powerful adult soon enough. Many exotic animals

are strong enough to be dangerous even without meaning to cause harm. An adult animal is also likely to be aggressive and have more difficult behaviors than a baby one.

**Wild animals are wild, even in captivity.** A dog is an animal, but it is a *domesticated* one—a species that has evolved over thousands of years to live well with people. Most dogs can be trained with a few puppy obedience classes. Exotic animals are something else entirely. They are wild animals with wild animal instincts, even when born in captivity. A wild animal is never 100 percent predictable. An animal that has behaved one way for many years cannot suddenly change. Domestication is not something that happens in one or two generations: it takes hundreds or thousands of years.

**Do you really have the resources?** If keeping a dog or cat can be time consuming and costly, that's nothing compared to looking after an adult lion or chimpanzee. It's not just the food and the vet bills, although those can indeed be considerable. You also have to build a sturdy cage or enclosure that is the appropriate size and has the right hiding, resting, climbing, and play spaces to approximate the animal's natural habitat. You will need to be able to devote a large portion of your time to learning about the animal and its needs. Usually only specially trained and qualified individuals working with the backing of a specially equipped facility are fully able to meet the needs of exotic animals. Keep in mind that pet ownership is a lifetime commitment. Jenny's dog may live to be 15, but a chimpanzee can live to be 60 or 65 years old.

**Dangers and Diseases.** While it is true that even dogs and cats can injure their owners or other people, they do not have the same unpredictable potential for serious or even deadly attacks that many exotic pets do. It's not just big cats, poisonous snakes, and chimpanzees that can be harmful—even smaller exotic pets can cause serious injuries. Exotic pets can also spread diseases to humans. In addition, many exotic pets end up on the loose in the wild. (Owners who find their fully-grown pets unmanageable sometimes release them.) Out on their own, these exotic animals can be a further danger to the public, and even to the environment.

**Cruel and Unusual.** Many exotic pet owners end up being unable to provide the proper living environment for their fully-grown pets. In order to prevent them from injuring anyone, they may decide to keep them caged. The end result is that far too many of these exotic animals spend almost their entire lives in the "prison" of a small cage. In this kind of environment, they have no opportunity to practice most of their "natural" behaviors.

All in all, Jenny is better off sticking with a "boring" dog or cat. If I were her parents, I'd say yes to the puppy before she got any more "exotic" ideas!

**Am I on Track?**

Actual Time Spent Reading

# SOURCE #2:
# REXANO Proves That Politicians and Lobbyists
## Introducing and Passing Laws Against Exotic Animal Ownership in the Name of 'Public Safety' Use False and Misleading Claims

Private owners of wild and exotic animals in the USA have been coming under ever increasing attacks from animal rights (AR) activists and uninformed legislators to end the private ownership of exotics in the name of "public safety." Many unfair laws have already passed on the federal, state and local levels.

REXANO (Responsible Exotic Animal Ownership), a free web resource designed to give facts-based research material to private owners of exotics to fight unfair legislation, just finished compiling a statistical table proving the legislators passing laws under the guise of
10 public safety used misleading claims.

"In the last 10–16 years, 1.5 people on average gets killed yearly by captive reptile, 1 by captive big cat, 0.81 by captive elephant, 0.125 by captive bear and 0 by captive nonhuman primate," reports Zuzana Kukol, a REXANO co-founder. "As a comparison, 45,000 people die each year in traffic accidents, 47 from lightning and 1,600 by falling down stairs."

"Our statistical analysis of the data disproves the claim that exotic animals in captivity are a threat to public safety. No uninvolved public has ever been killed in the USA since 1990 as a
20 result of a captive big cat, primate, bear, elephant or reptile at large," adds Scott Shoemaker, a REXANO co-founder. "The majority of fatalities are to owners, trainers or people voluntarily visiting the property where the animals are kept."

"If it is illegal for businesses to advertise and sell products using misleading and fraudulent claims, why is it OK for legislators and lobbyists to introduce, gain public support and pass bills using fraudulent claims they can't back up with facts?" asks Kukol. "These bills that waste tax money are appeasing the minority of special interest animal rights groups and a few individuals falling for the
30 claims of imaginary threats at the expense of constitutional freedoms for a majority of Americans. Many animal businesses are regulated out of existence as a result of this deception."

"There are no hard facts and statistics to support the case for these bans, only so-called incident reports compiled by the various AR groups," says Andrew Wyatt, President of NC Association of Reptile Keepers. "These incident reports amount to scary stories about scary animals. Many are unconfirmed, manufactured or ridiculous. Deaths or serious injuries are exceedingly rare. The reality is that you are more likely to contract *E. coli* virus from eating

40 spinach, and die as a result, than die from being attacked by an exotic animal."

"It would be nice if for once the AR fanatics could refrain from exploiting isolated tragic incidents, but they never do. They feed on this kind of hysteria," says Feline Conservation Federation president Lynn Culver. "AR groups use grieving relatives of those harmed by exotic animals as their poster children to help push their agenda of prohibiting exotic animals in society."

"Fear trumps over freedom. Will America be coerced by inflammatory rhetoric from the AR Movement into over reacting to

50 a nonexistent threat by enacting overly intrusive animal bans? I hope not," adds Wyatt.

"Animals are personal property; and we oppose legislation that restricts the private ownership or use of animals, or that inhibits free trade of any animal provided it meets Ohio Department of Agriculture testing and import requirements," adds Polly Britton, Secretary of the Ohio Association of Animal Owners.

"As long as animal welfare and public safety laws are followed, the private ownership of all animals should be protected in the USA," says Shoemaker.

60 "Control the land and the animals, then you control the people," states Kim Bloomer a natural pet care educator, lecturer and host of the online radio show Animal Talk Naturally.

"There is a hidden agenda with regard to all of these laws and it has nothing to do with public safety or concerns for good animal care. Rather, it is about eroding or removing American freedoms, the right to own as many animals as we can provide for."

Current focus of REXANO is to reverse the trend in over regulation.

**Am I on Track?**

Actual Time Spent Reading

# Part 1 Questions

Answer the following questions. You may refer to your reading notes, and you should cite text evidence in your responses. You will be able to refer to your answers as you write your essay in Part 2.

**1** Read this sentence from Source #2.

"These bills that waste tax money are appeasing the minority of special interest animal rights groups and a few individuals falling for the claims of imaginary threats at the expense of constitutional freedoms for a majority of Americans."

Based on the context of the sentence, which word has the same meaning as *appeasing*?

**a.** shocking

**b.** provoking

**c.** pacifying

**d.** applauding

**2** **Prose Constructed-Response** What are some of the obstacles owners of exotic pets face? Support your response with details from both sources.

_____

_____

_____

_____

**3** **Prose Constructed-Response** Briefly summarize the reasons why REXANO opposes bans on individuals owning exotic pets. Paraphrase information from Source #2 without plagiarizing.

_____

_____

_____

_____

_____

_____

# ▶ Part 2 (85 minutes)

You now have 85 minutes to review your notes and sources, and to plan, draft, edit, and revise your essay. While you may use your notes and refer to the sources, your essay must represent your original work. You may refer to your responses to Part 1 questions, but you cannot change those answers. Now read your assignment and the information about how your writing will be scored; then begin your work.

## Your Assignment

It is time to start writing the argumentative essay on exotic pets that you will send to the community newspaper. Remember, your essay should explain whether you agree or disagree that private citizens should be allowed to keep exotic animals as pets. When writing your essay, find ways to use information from the two sources to support your argument. A good argumentative essay should include a strong claim, and it should address opposing arguments.

## Argumentative Essay Scoring

Your essay will be scored using the following:

1. **Organization/purpose:** How well did you express your claim, address opposing claims, and support your claim with logical ideas? How well did your ideas flow from beginning to end? How effective was your introduction and conclusion?

2. **Evidence/elaboration:** How well did you incorporate relevant information from the sources? Did you use specific titles or numbers in referring to the sources? How strong is the elaboration for your ideas? Did you clearly state your ideas in your own words in a way that is appropriate for your audience and purpose?

3. **Conventions:** How well did you follow the rules of grammar, punctuation, capitalization, and spelling?

**Now begin work on your essay.** Manage your time carefully so that you can:

- plan your essay, using your notes

- write your essay

- revise and edit your final draft

# TASK 2

**RESEARCH SIMULATION**

# *Informative Essay*

You are a member of a community service club at your school. The club has decided to do a public awareness campaign about staying safe during outdoor activities.

First you will review two articles about the dangers of hiking alone. After you have reviewed these sources, you will answer some questions about them. You should first skim the sources and the questions and then go back and read them carefully.

In Part 2, you will write an informative essay in which you explain why it is important for hikers to communicate their plans before leaving.

# Time Management: Informative Task

There are two parts to most formal writing tests. Both parts of the tests are timed, so it's important to use your limited time wisely.

## Part 1: Read Sources and Answer Questions

### Preview the Assignment

35 minutes

You will have 35 minutes to read two sources about hiking outdoors. You will also answer questions about the sources.

*35 minutes! That's not much time.*

### How Many?

*Preview the questions. This will help you know which information you'll need to find as you read.*

How many pages of reading?

How many multiple-choice questions?

How many prose constructed-response questions?

### How do you plan to use the 35 minutes?

*Underline, circle, and take notes as you read. You probably won't have time to reread.*

Estimated time to read:

*This is a lot to do in a short time.*

Source #1: "Miraculous Lost and Found"                    minutes

Source #2: "The Most Important Rule"                    minutes

Estimated time to answer questions?                    minutes

**Total**                                     **35    minutes**

### Any concerns?

_____

_____

_____

_____

_____

## Part 2: Write the Essay

**85**

*How much time do you have? Pay attention to the clock!*

**Plan and Write an Informative Essay**

85 minutes

You will have 85 minutes to plan, write, revise, and edit your essay.

**Your Plan**

Before you start writing, think about the main idea of your essay. What is the most important point you need to make?

_____

_____

**How do you plan to use the 85 minutes?**

| | |
|---|---|
| Estimated time for planning the essay? | [ ] minutes |
| Estimated time for writing? | [ ] minutes |
| Estimated time for editing? | [ ] minutes |
| Estimated time for checking spelling, grammar, punctuation? | [ ] minutes |
| **Total** | **85 minutes** |

*Be sure to leave enough time for this step.*

**Notes:**

_____

_____

_____

_____

*Reread your essay, making sure that the points are clear. Check that there are no spelling or punctuation mistakes.*

## ▶ Your Task

As part of a community service project, you are to write an informative essay for the public about hiking safety. In researching the topic, you have identified two sources you will use in planning your essay.

After you have reviewed the sources, you will answer some questions about them. Briefly skim the sources and the three questions that follow. Then, go back and read the sources carefully so you will have the information you will need to answer the questions. Take notes on the sources as you read. You may refer back to your notes at any time during Part 1 or Part 2 of the performance task.

## ▶ Part 1 (35 minutes)

You will now read the sources. After carefully reading the sources, use the rest of the time in Part 1 to answer the three questions about them. Though your answers to these questions will help you think about what you have read and plan your essay, they will also be scored as part of the test.

SOURCE #1:
THE WAYNE COUNTY GAZETTE

# Miraculous Lost and Found

**by Katherine Leonard,**
*Staff Writer*

*Friday, May 2, 2003*

Aron Ralston, a mountaineer from Aspen, Colorado, lost for over five days in Blue John Canyon, was miraculously found alive yesterday. The experienced climber had been trapped by a big boulder that came loose and pinned his arm against the wall of a narrow canyon that he was descending. Ralston was able to free himself by amputating his arm with a multi-tool pocket knife.

The Meijers, a Dutch family that was hiking in the park, saw Ralston walking aimlessly a few hours after he performed the amputation and immediately gave him food and water, and alerted
10  a rescue team that was already in the area looking for the missing climber.

The authorities are putting together the pieces that form this incredible survival story as more details of Ralston's ordeal surface. It seems that the Colorado climber was mountain-biking in the Canyonlands National Park, when he put down his bike to take a closer look at a very narrow canyon. As he was climbing down, the boulder, with a reported weight of 800 pounds, broke loose and, rolling down, got stuck, pinning Ralston's arm against the wall. Ralston had not told anyone where he was going, or when he
20  expected to return, making a disastrous situation much, much worse.

Slowly consuming the only food he had to eat, two burritos, and taking small sips of his remaining water (about 350 ml), the mountaineer spent the majority of four days waiting for somebody to find him. On his fourth night, he is said to have had an epiphany— amputation was his only way to survive. No one knew he was missing. He would have to rescue himself.

Ralston spent several hours using a dull knife to cut his own arm at the radius. Once free, he rappelled down a 65-foot wall with one hand and started walking the 8 miles that separated him from his car. It was then the Meijer family found him and got help. Ralston was taken to a hospital in Grand Junction, Co., where he remains in critical condition. "He was in pretty rough shape but he communicated with us all the way to the hospital," said the Emery County sheriff Mitch Vetere. "He is obviously a tough guy." Ralston had lost 40 pounds and quite a bit of blood by the time he got to the hospital.

30

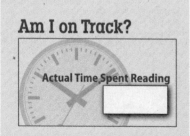

# The Most Important Rule

by Jared Myers

As any good adventurist knows, there are a number of common-sense rules to follow when engaging in a successful hike: bring plenty of water, dress appropriately, map out the trail you will be hiking in advance, and be sure to bring along a first aid kit. However, the most important rule of hiking is also one of the most commonly overlooked: Alert a family member or friend to the location of your proposed hike and an estimated time of return.

While any amount of advance planning or familiarity with a particular hiking trail may seem to be an adequate substitute for
10  alerting a friend or loved one, rarely does this planning or familiarity account for an emergency. These unexpected difficulties can come in many forms, including swiftly deteriorating weather conditions, an encounter with dangerous wildlife, or even something as small as a sprained ankle.

For example, in an effort to follow in the footsteps of hiker Aron Ralston, 64-year-old Amos Wayne Richards made an attempt to traverse Utah's Blue John Canyon in September of 2011. However, after falling 10 feet, Richards dislocated his shoulder and shattered his leg. With only two protein bars, an empty water bottle, no family
20  or friends aware of his hiking plans, and no cell phone service with which to contact them, Richards began to drag himself back to his car along the rocky terrain. Four days later, rangers set off to rescue him, tipped off by the discovery of his abandoned campsite and truck. From clues at the campsite and from conversations with Richard's family and friends, rangers figured out where he was likely located and dispatched a helicopter. After using the flash on his camera to catch the attention of the pilot, Amos Wayne Richards was treated for his broken leg and for dehydration at a nearby hospital before being released. The whole ordeal, however, could have been
30  prevented, had he simply informed a friend or family member of his hiking plans and his estimated time of return.

New advancements in technology have made it easier for hikers to plan for unexpected emergencies in advance, without worrying their friends and family unnecessarily. HikerAlert, a web-based service, allows you to enter your hiking itinerary and projected

**NOTES**

return time into its database before your departure. If you fail to respond to a text from the HikerAlert website, checking in with you at your projected return time, a text is sent to your designated emergency contacts entered when the account was created, encouraging them to attempt to contact you.

40

It's easy to understand why someone may feel it unnecessary to reach out to friends and family before going out on a new adventure. For some, admitting the possibility of danger may make them feel like they appear to be weak or inexperienced. Others may feel that their friends or family may worry too much about them while they are away. However, following this one simple rule may ultimately save your life and ensure that the next hike you go on won't be your last.

**Am I on Track?**

Actual Time Spent Reading

# Part 1 Questions

**Answer the following questions. You may refer to your reading notes, and you should cite text evidence in your responses. Your answers to these questions will be scored. You will be able to refer to your answers as you write your essay in Part 2.**

**1** Choose two important pieces of safety advice from the sources and explain why each is important. Support your response with quotations from the sources.

_____

_____

_____

_____

_____

**2** Which of the following sentences best states an accurate claim one could make after reading these selections?

   **a.** Amos Wayne Richards's accident was unrelated to Aron Ralston's accident.

   **b.** The Meijer family found Aron Ralston because they were aware of his location.

   **c.** Aron Ralston did not have enough experience as a hiker to know what he was getting into.

   **d.** Technology can be an important asset for hikers who do not want to cause unnecessary worry.

**3** Which piece of evidence best supports your answer to Question 2?

   **a.** "... a text is sent to your designated emergency contacts entered when the account was created ..." (Source #2, lines 38–39)

   **b.** "... 64-year-old Amos Wayne Richards made an attempt to traverse Utah's Blue John Canyon ..." (Source #2, lines 16–17)

   **c.** "Once free, he rappelled down a 65-foot wall with one hand ..." (Source #1, lines 28–29)

   **d.** "The experienced climber had been trapped by a big boulder that came loose and pinned his arm against the wall of a narrow canyon that he was descending." (Source #1, lines 3–5)

# ▶ Part 2 (85 minutes)

You have 85 minutes to review your notes and sources, and to plan, draft, edit, and revise your essay. While you may use your notes and refer to the sources, your work must represent your original work. You may refer to your responses to Part 1 questions, but you cannot change those answers. Now read your assignment and the information about how your writing will be scored; then begin your work.

## Your Assignment

It is time to start writing your informative essay on hiking safety for the community service club. Your essay should explain why it is important for hikers to communicate their hiking plans before leaving. When writing your essay, find ways to use information from the two sources to support your thesis. Be sure to present your ideas in a logical order.

## Informative Essay Scoring

Your essay will be scored using the following:

1. **Organization/purpose:** How well did you state your thesis and support your thesis with a logical progression of ideas? Did you use a variety of transitions between ideas? Was your focus narrow enough to lead to a well-formed conclusion?

2. **Evidence/elaboration:** How well did you incorporate relevant information from the sources? How well did you elaborate your ideas? Did you use precise language appropriate to your audience and purpose?

3. **Conventions:** How well did you follow the rules of grammar, punctuation, capitalization, and spelling?

**Now begin work on your essay.** Manage your time carefully so that you can:

- plan your essay, using your notes

- write your essay

- revise and edit your final draft

# TASK 3

# Literary Analysis

Your language arts teacher has assigned your class a literary analysis of two poems. Both of these poems are about Helen of Troy, who plays an important role in the literature of Ancient Greece.

First you will review the two poems. After you have reviewed these sources, you will answer some questions about them. You should first skim the sources and the questions and then go back and read them carefully.

In Part 2, you will write a literary analysis in which you compare and contrast poems by the American poets Edgar Allan Poe and H.D. (Hilda Doolittle).

# Time Management: Literary Analysis Task

Most formal writing tests are made up of two parts. Both parts of the tests are timed, so it's important to use your limited time wisely.

## Part 1: Read Sources and Answer Questions

### Preview the Assignment

35 minutes

You will have 35 minutes to read two poems to discover how the same subject, Helen of Troy, is treated differently in the two sources. You will also answer questions about each source.

> 35 minutes! That's not much time.

### How Many?

> Preview the questions. This will help you know which information you'll need to find as you read.

How many pages of reading?

How many multiple-choice questions?

How many prose constructed-response questions?

### How do you plan to use the 35 minutes?

> Underline, circle, and take notes as you read. You probably won't have time to reread.

> This is a lot to do in a short time.

Estimated time to read:

Source #1: "To Helen"                    _____ minutes

Source #2: "Helen"                        _____ minutes

Estimated time to answer questions?       _____ minutes

**Total**                         **35**  **minutes**

### Any concerns?

_____

_____

_____

_____

_____

# Part 2: Write the Analysis

*How much time do you have? Pay attention to the clock!*

## Plan and Write a Literary Analysis

**85 minutes**

You will have 85 minutes to plan, write, revise, and edit your literary analysis.

## Your Plan

Before you start writing, decide how you will organize your literary analysis:

Point-by-Point? ☐            Subject-by-Subject? ☐

## How do you plan to use the 85 minutes?

| | | |
|---|---|---|
| Estimated time for planning the essay? | | minutes |
| Estimated time for writing? | | minutes |
| Estimated time for editing? | | minutes |
| Estimated time for checking spelling, grammar, punctuation? | | minutes |
| **Total** | **85** | **minutes** |

*Be sure to leave enough time for this step.*

## Notes:

_____

_____

_____

_____

*Reread your essay, making sure that the points are clear. Check that there are no spelling or punctuation mistakes.*

## ► Your Task

> You have been assigned a literary analysis of poems by
> Edgar Allan Poe and H.D. You will analyze these two sources
> and write an essay that compares and contrasts the way
> each poem treats the subject common to both, which is
> Helen of Troy.

After you have reviewed the sources, you will answer some questions about
them. Briefly skim the sources and the questions that follow. Then, go back
and read the sources carefully so you will have the information you will need
to answer the questions. Take notes on the sources as you read. You may refer
back to your notes at any time during Part 1 or Part 2 of the performance task.

## ► Part 1 (35 minutes)

You will now read the sources. After carefully reading the sources, use the rest
of the time in Part 1 to answer the five questions about them. Though your
answers to these questions will help you think about what you have read and
plan your literary analysis, they will also be scored as part of the test.

## SOURCE #1:

# To Helen

**by Edgar Allan Poe**

Helen, thy beauty is to me
    Like those Nicéan barks of yore,
That gently, o'er a perfumed sea,
    The weary, way-worn wanderer bore
5    To his own native shore.°

On desperate seas long wont to roam,
    Thy hyacinth hair, thy classic face,
Thy Naiad° airs have brought me home
    To the glory that was Greece,
10    And the grandeur that was Rome.

Lo! in yon brilliant window-niche
    How statuelike I see thee stand,
The agate lamp within thy hand!
    Ah, Psyche,° from the regions which
15    Are Holy Land!

---

5. **Nicéan . . . shore:** Nicea was a Greek colony; the wanderer referred to is Odysseus.
8. **Naiad:** nymphlike.
14. **Psyche:** mortal woman whose great beauty captivated Cupid, the god of Love.

**NOTES**

**Am I on Track?**

Actual Time Spent Reading

# SOURCE #2:
# Helen

### by H.D.

All Greece hates
the still eyes in the white face,
the luster as of olives
where she stands,
5   and the white hands.

All Greece reviles
the wan face when she smiles,
hating it deeper still
when it grows wan and white,
10   remembering past enchantments
       and past ills.

Greece sees unmoved,
God's daughter,° born of love,
the beauty of cool feet
15   and slenderest knees,
could love indeed the maid,
only if she were laid,
white ash amid funereal cypresses.

---

13. **God's daughter:** Helen was a daughter of Zeus, the king of the gods. She was conceived when Zeus (in the form of a swan) seduced the mortal Leda.

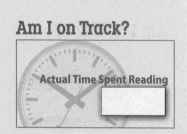

# Part 1 Questions

Answer the following questions. You may refer to your reading notes, and you should cite text evidence in your responses. Your answers to these questions will be scored. You will be able to refer to your answers as you write your essay in Part 2.

**1** What does the word *barks* most likely mean in these lines from Source #1?

> "Helen, thy beauty is to me
>> Like those Nicéan barks of yore,
> That gently, o'er a perfumed sea,
>> The weary, way-worn wanderer bore
>> To his own native shore."
>
> (lines 1–5)

- **a.** harsh sounds
- **b.** sailors
- **c.** outer covering of trees
- **d.** ships

**2** Which word (or phrase) from Source #1 in Question 1 best helps you understand the meaning of *barks*?

- **a.** "Nicéan"
- **b.** "way-worn wanderer"
- **c.** "o'er a perfumed sea"
- **d.** "gently"

**3** Which of the following sentences best states an important difference between the two poems concerning their depiction of Helen of Troy?

- **a.** In contrast to Source #1, Source #2 celebrates Helen for her classic beauty.
- **b.** The speaker in Source #1 compares Helen to a "weary, way-worn wanderer," whereas in Source #2 the speaker compares her to a lifeless statue.
- **c.** In Source #1, Helen is worshiped for her beauty, whereas in Source #2, her face is detested by the Greeks.
- **d.** Although both sources draw attention to Helen's face, Source #1 treats it as an example of classic beauty, whereas Source #2 depicts it as fierce and savage.

4. Select two pieces of evidence from Source #1 and two pieces of evidence from Source #2 that support your answer to Question 3.

   **a.** "Helen, thy beauty is to me / Like those Nicéan barks of yore . . ." (Source #1, lines 1–2)

   **b.** "That gently, o'er a perfumed sea, / The weary, way-worn wanderer bore . . ." (Source #1, lines 3–4)

   **c.** "Thy hyacinth hair, thy classic face, / Thy Naiad airs have brought me home . . ." (Source #1, lines 7–8)

   **d.** "Lo! in yon brilliant window-niche / How statuelike I see thee stand . . ." (Source #1, lines 11–12)

   **e.** "All Greece hates / the still eyes in the white face . . ." (Source #2, lines 1–2)

   **f.** "All Greece reviles / the wan face when she smiles . . ." (Source #2, lines 6–7)

   **g.** "God's daughter, born of love . . ." (Source #2, line 13)

   **h.** "the beauty of cool feet / and slenderest knees . . ." (Source #2, lines 14–15)

5. **Prose Constructed-Response** According to Source #2, what do the people of Greece think of Helen? Cite specific evidence from the text in your response.

_____

_____

_____

_____

_____

_____

_____

_____

_____

_____

_____

_____

# ▶ Part 2 (85 minutes)

You will have 85 minutes to review your notes and sources, and to plan, draft, edit, and revise your essay. While you may use your notes and refer to the sources, your essay must represent your original work. You may refer to your responses to Part 1, but you cannot change those answers. Now read your assignment and the information about how your writing will be scored; then begin your work.

## Your Assignment

It's time to begin your literary analysis. Think about the two poems and what you want to say about them. As you write your essay, compare and contrast the treatment of Helen of Troy in the sources. Make sure that you include quotations from both poems and that you present your ideas in a logical order.

## Literary Analysis Scoring

Your literary analysis will be scored using the following:

1. **Organization/purpose:** How well did you state your thesis/controlling idea and support it with a logical progression of ideas? Did you use a variety of transitions between ideas? Was your controlling idea narrow enough to lead to a logical conclusion?

2. **Evidence/elaboration:** How well did you incorporate relevant information from the literary texts? How well did you elaborate your ideas? Did you use precise language appropriate to your audience and purpose?

3. **Conventions:** How well did you follow the rules of grammar, punctuation, capitalization, and spelling?

**Now begin work on your literary analysis.** Manage your time carefully so that you can:

- plan your essay, using your notes
- write your essay
- revise and edit your final draft

# Acknowledgments

"Helen" from *Collected Poems 1912–1944* by H.D. Text copyright © 1982 by the Estate of Hilda Doolittle. Reprinted by permission of New Directions Publishing Corporation and Carcanet.

"REXANO Proves Politicians and Lobbyists Introducing and Passing Laws Against Exotic Animal Ownership in the Name of 'Public Safety' Use False and Misleading Claims" from *PRWeb,* March 17, 2007, www. prweb.com. Text copyright © 2007 by Rexano. Reprinted by permission of Rexano.

"Social Media, Pretend Friends, and the Lie of False Intimacy" by Jay Baer from *Convince & Convert,* www.convinceandconvert.com. Text copyright © 2008-2013 by Convince & Convert, LLC. Reprinted by permission of Convince & Convert, LLC.

"Spring is like a perhaps hand" from *Complete Poems: 1904–1962* by E. E. Cummings. Text copyright © 1923, 1925, 1951, 1953, 1991 by the Trustees for the E. E. Cummings Trust. Text copyright © 1976 by George James Firmage. Reprinted by permission of Liveright Publishing Corporation.

"Study: The Internet Helps You Make More Friends, Be More Social" by Graeme McMillan from *Time,* June 16, 2011, www.techland.time.com. Text copyright © 2011 by Time, Inc. Reprinted by permission of Time, Inc.